HOW TO START & SCALE AN AIRBNB BUSINESS WITHOUT OWNING PROPERTY

BEGINNERS GUIDE TO MARKETING YOUR LISTINGS, MAKING A PROFIT IN 9 DAYS & GENERATING A PASSIVE INCOME

KAY CARROLL

CONTENTS

INTRODUCTION

My first Airbnb experience was a stylish one-bedroom condo in Boston's Jeffries Point Neighborhood. I was en route to London but needed to stop in Boston for business.

My assistant recommended that I look into private housing. When she searched for hotels, she found many were too far from the airport, too rundown, or too expensive. She sent me photos of a modern one-bedroom condo with everything I could possibly need, from luxurious finishes to a private deck. The condo was about 600 square feet, so a tad on the smaller side but just right for my stay. It was steps to Piers Park with breathtaking views of Boston's skyline and a five-minute train ride downtown.

Booking it was a no-brainer.

My host emailed to inform me he was away and his sister would be there to hand me the keys. His sister enthusiastically walked me through the condo. She explained how her brother intended to pay off the mortgage by renting it out on a yearly basis. However, he realized he could earn more money by leasing it for short stays. Even accounting for times the condo was vacant.

On the day I left Boston, the owner was back in the city and took me to the airport. We talked as we drove. He frequently traveled for work, lived in the condo while in the city, and stayed at her sister's place when it was rented. Today, the American dream of home ownership is a fantasy for many young people. At 22, he was a homeowner and earning a living.

My second Airbnb experience came a few months later. I was surfing with a group in Malaita, one of the spectacular Solomon Islands. The group had limited lodging options, and I wanted my own room with a shower. It was in a young couple's four-bedroom house, a short distance from the site.

The husband was employed, and the wife stayed at home to raise their children. Due to a lack of money, they listed the spare room for short-term rentals. Despite not being able to afford to travel, they wanted their young children's minds to be open to diverse backgrounds and experiences.

Airbnb was a complete accident, but I quickly became addicted. Regardless of where I am, I am able to stay in a place that fulfills my requirements. When I travel for pleasure, I enjoy being in the center of things, but sans the chaos of a city hotel. I can rent a place that is more unique and luxurious at the same price or less than a nearby hotel.

I am currently scouting Airbnb for a vacation rental for some friends and I. There are about ten of us, including small kids. It is important for us to be together without spending a fortune on a hotel that cannot guarantee connecting or even rooms on the same floor.

I've always been annoyed by the response I get from hotels when I request connecting rooms for a big group getaway. "We will take your wishes into consideration, but we cannot promise connecting rooms up front." Booking your dream room is like winning the jackpot. Airbnb takes the risk out of it. You get what you pay for. If the rental fails to live up to your expectations, you can rely on Airbnb. They are committed to transparency and integrity.

In 1998, I started my first side business selling my old toys on eBay at 10. I have been addicted ever since and now own & run multiple businesses that generate passive income. The idea of investing in short-term rentals appealed to me. Once I got started, I never looked back! Airbnb arbitrage has been one of my most profitable and fastest-growing lines of business.

Since its inception, Airbnb has grown to provide a number of options to earn income on the platform beyond owning properties and renting them out. *Airbnb Arbitrage* is a popular practice among entrepreneurs who want to start an Airbnb business without owning any property. This strategy allows hosts to sublet rented spaces to Airbnb guests.

I started my Airbnb rental arbitrage business in a time of financial crisis. Financially strained and worried about paying my rent, I listed my home on Airbnb. The rent on the house was $2,000 monthly, so if I put it on the platform for $3,000, Airbnb profits would cover my rent and leave me with $1,000, not including any upkeep fees.

Immediately, I saw that the strategy had tremendous income potential, and the seed for my Airbnb arbitrage business was sown. Within a year, I earned more than five figures per month from ten listings. However, unlike most hosts, I did not own a property. Even though my business is thriving today, it wasn't always easy. Airbnb arbitrage involves preparing, finding a reliable property owner, decorating the property, and optimizing it on Airbnb for the best visibility.

Renting out a room or a home that you are leasing can provide financial security. No deposits. No loans. It gives you the opportunity to generate income without the hassles and responsibilities of home ownership. This is the precise reason I started my Airbnb business. Today, I am one of the top earners on Airbnb, making a full-time income through just my Airbnb business.

I'm here to help you learn practical tips for succeeding as an Airbnb business-owner: everything I wish I knew back then. You don't need to live in a tourist destination or have a fancy rental to earn money as a host. Of course, guests will shell-out big bucks for a five-star stay, but there's something for everyone. Airbnb arbitrage has proven to be highly profitable for short-term rental investors. It's a favorite among investors seeking financial independence through passive income.

Many would-be investors are skeptical of Airbnb arbitrage. Of course, there is always a risk, so first-time Airbnb hosts need to learn the ropes before diving right in. Be patient and think long-term.

Is it profitable? What are the steps to get started? How do I find the properties? If you're ready to start an Airbnb rental business without actually owning property, welcome aboard the hosting express.

1

HOW AIRBNB BECAME A
"UNICORN" IN SILICON VALLEY

Airbnb did not pioneer private lodging. Travelers have been using homestays as an alternative to traditional accommodations for decades, relying on a sign at the entrance, a mention in the newspaper, or the local tourism office.

Technology merely eased the process of connecting travelers with property owners. Platforms like Airbnb have revolutionized the hospitality industry globally by providing a platform where property owners and potential guests can connect; turning the hotel industry into a whirlwind.

Vacationers can choose from a variety of accommodations, from a potato hotel to a covered wagon to a downtown penthouse and everything in between.

Airbnb has changed the way we travel. While hotel chains struggle to stay relevant, Airbnb is booming.

The current estimated value of the short-term rental market is $74.64 billion and is projected to increase at a compound annual growth rate of 5.3% from 2022 to 2030 (Grand View Research, n.d.). Tourists from more than 200 countries rent private properties. Globally, the top-five hotel brands are Marriott International, Hilton Worldwide Holdings Inc., Intercontinental Hotels Group, Wyndham Worldwide Corp, and Hyatt Hotels Corporation. On any given night, Airbnb has more rooms available than the five largest hotel chains combined (Editor, 2017).

Everyday, hundreds of hosts join, and while the industry is far from crowded, demand for travelers is on the rise. Within certain regions, the industry is booming. There is still a lot of money to be made, but you need to first decide if Airbnb is right for you.

WHAT IS AIRBNB?

An email sparked everything. Joe Gebbia contacted Brian Chesky about a project. What if they turned their apartment into a B&B, complete with mattresses and breakfast? The idea was to earn a few dollars. Today, that concept is worth $38 billion. The two classmates at Rhode Island School of Design decided giving tours and housing to traveling artists was an entertaining way to earn extra income. They built a basic website, purchased three inflatable mattresses, and set them up in their apartment. They scored three guests, two men and a woman, who spent $80 each to sleep on air mattresses (Aydin, 2019).

Gebbia and Chesky soon realized the value of their concept. Nathan Blecharczyk, their former roommate, helped them turn it into a fully-functioning business. Four years after welcoming its first guest, Airbnb had expanded to 89 countries with 1 million nights booked. It was also awarded SXSW's Breakout Mobile App Award. Around the same time, venture capitalists invested $112 million in the startup, valuing it at more than $1 billion.

Today, countless hosts and vacationers use Airbnb to promote their homes and discover exceptional lodging around the world. Airbnb hosts offer a wide range of accommodations, from shared rooms to a deluxe French Polynesian "private atoll."

There are four types of rental spaces: entire properties, private rooms, hotel rooms, and shared spaces.

Private property: Access to an entire studio, apartment, or house. Your visitors will not share any space with you or others.

Private rooms: Visitors will have their own room and possibly their own bathroom. Guests may share a bathroom, kitchen, or living room with you or other travelers.

Hotel rooms: Whether private or communal, hotel rooms offer the amenities and comfort of a standard hotel. The rooms are located in upscale or luxury hotels, inns, B&Bs, or similar establishments. They usually feature attractive communal areas and suites with special features.

Shared space: Guests don't necessarily have their own rooms. If you like, you can offer a sleeping bag in your basement.

Simply put, you're renting out your place to strangers and not everyone is a fan. There are security concerns that you will have to face, as well as privacy and space concerns. Airbnb strives to make the entire process safe. During the last year, I have hosted over 700 guests at my various properties and have never encountered any problems.

Anyone using Airbnb is screened before they can book a stay or become a host. Various levels of verification can be completed, but the most basic requires that guests and hosts have their identity, address and phone number checked. Furthermore, Airbnb provides extensive insurance coverage to protect you from accidents and damage caused by your visitors.

Another benefit of Airbnb is that as a host you get to choose the arrival and departure times for your guests. Guests can negotiate check-in and check-out times with you, however, you have the option of accepting or rejecting requests. When I started out, I had a check-in time of 5pm or later so I could get home from my job. Today, I mostly work at home, so guests can come early, but I don't allow guests to arrive after 9pm. After staying up until dawn a few times waiting for guests to arrive, it eventually loses its appeal. Latecomers often miscalculated the distance or the time it will take. Of course, guests might experience flight delays and I'm still flexible in those instances.

Having someone stay in one of your spaces poses another issue, your freedom. Renting out your property means that, surprise, strangers will be staying in your rental. You will have nights where you would like to go out but cannot because guests will be arriving. However, from the perspective of someone who enjoys solitude for days, it becomes second nature. Meeting new people is a fulfilling experience and many of them return so you build great relationships, and you make great money.

AIRBNB SERVICE FEES

Airbnb charges hosts and travelers a service fee in return for advertising, management, and customer service.

The fee is calculated based on the total amount of each reservation. The fee is applied instantly so that hosts and guests know exactly what the cost of each stay will be prior to booking. Hosts can see the fee amount subtracted from their payout when viewing their Airbnb history, and guests will see it deducted when confirming their booking.

Airbnb offers two types of service fees: host-only fees and split-fees. Here are the main differences between the two.

The Split-Fee

To put it simply, the split-fee is split between the host and the guest, with the guest bearing most of the costs.

The upside to this model is that hosts can charge lower rates since they are not paying as much in fees. The main disadvantage is that guests may feel cheated if the charge only appears at checkout.

Guests are charged roughly 3% of the total amount of the booking, excluding taxes, under the split-fee system. Airbnb may bill a higher rate for Airbnb Plus hosts, those with rentals in Italy, and hosts with a strict cancellation policy.

With this fee structure, guests are responsible for the bulk of service fees. The guest fee typically comes to approximately 14% of the total reservation amount.

The Host-Only Fee

The host is responsible for covering the service charge under this fee model. While this may appear to be a less desirable choice for hosts, it ultimately gives you greater flexibility in pricing. Furthermore, guests are more satisfied when they are not stung with a service charge at check-out.

Fees are required for hotels and software-based hosts unless the majority of their listings are located in the USA, the Bahamas, Canada, Taiwan, Argentina, Mexico, or Uruguay. The host pays approximately 14-16% of the total amount of the booking. Travelers won't be billed a service charge, but hosts can increase their rates to effectively pass along the fee.

The platform's fees are unavoidable for hosts who use it. However, the cost you will have to pay varies based on where you live and the amount you allocate to guests.

Furthermore, there are ways to reduce or lessen the burden of the service fee, which I will cover in a moment. Let's begin by looking at why the Airbnb host-only service fee may be a good idea.

THE BENEFITS OF USING THE AIRBNB HOST-ONLY FEE STRUCTURE

The primary benefit of the host-only model is that you have increased flexibility over your business. Consequently, you gain these advantages:

Travelers Pay Less and Profits Remain the Same

Since hosts subtract service charges from their earnings, they can effectively manage their rates. By following a reasonable rate plan, guests can save money, and your profit will not change.

For instance, if you charge $200 per night with the split-fee, guests will pay the $2000 + $284 service charge for a stay of 10 nights, totaling $2284. There will be a $60 service fee in this scenario, so you'll have $1940 left over.

On the other hand, if you choose the host-only fee, you can increase your nightly rate to $226 to cover Airbnb fees that you are well aware of. During the 10-night stay, guests will pay a total of $2260, which is lower than in the Airbnb split-fee scenario. If you are charged a service charge of 14%, Airbnb will deduct about $316 from your payout, leaving you with a take-home revenue of $1684. While it may decrease your profit slightly, it will increase your occupancy rate, so it's worth it and in the long run your overall profit will be higher.

Travelers Won't be Surprised With Extra Fees

With this model, since Airbnb only takes a cut of the host's earnings, guests won't feel cheated or surprised by additional charges tacked on at checkout. It is a much better experience for guests if they are billed the amount expected and you, as the host, take care of the service charge behind the scenes.

Rank Higher in Airbnb's Search Results

Airbnb promotes properties that improve the guest experience by boosting their exposure. The host-only fee makes reservations more effortless and more trustworthy for guests. In turn, Airbnb favors hosts by ranking them higher in search results.

YOU CAN MAKE INSANE PROFITS EVEN WITH AIRBNB FEES

Although you will pay AirBnB fees while operating your company, you can still increase your profits. Here are some ways to maximize your Airbnb income even after paying service fees.

Nail Your Pricing Rate

In order to increase your earnings, the smartest approach is to ensure that your rates are competitive and that your property is generating as much profit as possible. As you determine your price, remember to include Airbnb's fee and other significant overhead costs while still keeping it reasonable. Setting the right price can be challenging. Fortunately, some services can help you determine your pricing.

Dynamic pricing tools can help you simplify the process of pricing your rental. These programs can analyze current market conditions, pricing patterns, and price changes to adjust your rental prices automatically and give you the edge over your competitors. While dynamic pricing tools can be expensive, they are well worth the cost if they increase your profits. We'll provide details on the various tools that you can use later in this book.

Boost Your Occupancy

The more reservations you get, the higher your profits will be. Your fees will be more than covered if you can increase occupancy and keep your rates low. Similarly, when occupancy is low, every booking becomes more precious, and letting hefty Airbnb fees cut into your revenue will hurt.

If you want to increase your rental rate, here are some things to consider:

- Update your property details regularly
- Optimize your advertising efforts
- Attract glowing reviews from guest
- Respond to potential guest questions quickly
- Use the Instant Booking feature

Make Use of Airbnb Management Software

When managing multiple Airbnb properties, it is easy to become overwhelmed by the workload. Using these tools can simplify workflow, prevent duplicate bookings, and reduce expenses. Airbnb arbitrage becomes much easier. Instead of focusing on the backend of your business, you can direct your attention to creating a positive guest experience, ultimately leading to better reviews and more profits.

Don't Implement the Super Strict Cancellation fee

Airbnb's fees vary based on the cancellation policy. Hosts who implement the "Super Strict" cancellation policy will incur 2% extra in fees because of the additional paperwork and support required. You can opt for another cancellation policy if you want lower service fees.

Add a Cleaning fee

Airbnb lets hosts include cleaning charges in the rental price. A cleaning fee helps offset your expenses in keeping your place clean and inviting. You won't have to take money out of profits to pay for these costs, which will leave more money in your pockets.

This will raise guest booking totals. Don't charge so much that you are no longer affordable and guests are tempted to find another place to stay. Keep your cleaning fee in line with the industry average of $65 per reservation.

Provide Extra Amenities to Travelers

Providing extra amenities to guests is an excellent way to garner positive reviews from guests and in turn, increase profits through more bookings. When potential guests read about the amazing experiences that others have had at your property, then you'll certainly get more bookings. Additional amenities include items and services that enhance your guests' experience. For instance, you might offer luxury toiletries, pet-friendly accommodation, or spa services for an additional fee. Furthermore, you can provide food or organize excursions and adventures in your city.

On Airbnb's platform, service charges cannot be avoided. It's important to remember that Airbnb is the industry leader, with a substantial number of properties and a wide reach. You have the opportunity to reach a large number of travelers — something you would not be able to do without the platform.

Vacationers are often trustworthy people, and no matter where they go, they want to see the attractions, make new friends, and not trash your place. Using Airbnb is a simple way to renew your trust in mankind once you see that most guests respect your property and won't destroy it. In the event that they did, Airbnb would compensate you and would most likely get the authorities involved. In addition, said guests wouldn't be able to use the platform again, which is the last thing a passionate traveler wants.

Nevertheless, incidents will occur, and there will be more load on rugs, bathrooms, and vacuums. You'll probably need to invest more time cleaning towels and sheets. However, it is a way to earn money from an asset that you do not own. It is not a get-rich-quick or a pyramid scheme, but a clever way to start a real estate business without owning property.

AIRBNB EXPERIENCES

Airbnb has broadened its services with a service called Airbnb Experiences. This service was launched in 2016 and provides a unique experience for Airbnb customers. In addition, it's also creating a potential stream of income for Airbnb hosts.

Guests can book Airbnb Experiences during their stay. Hosts will guide these experiences. These are not conventional sightseeing tours or workshops. Anybody with an artistic interest or passion is welcome to participate in the service.

Airbnb Experiences aren't limited to a particular service. People use it to connect with others, and some find local events through it. Experiences draw interest from group and solo travelers alike.

An experience may include anything from a coffee masterclass to a Tango concert. It must be more than a standard tour people can book from an operator. Airbnb does not restrict what hosts can do, but they must be in charge. Experiences can be a few hours to several days.

Please note that this is a separate service from Airbnb property hosting. Hosts looking to offer activities do not need to accommodate overnight guests. Hosts can also list their services at any time without any limitations.

Both platforms share one thing: the need for a license. Particularly if an experience includes meals, drinks, or travel.

Airbnb hosts cannot offer experiences without being vetted by Airbnb. To participate, hosts are required to apply. They will then be notified by Airbnb whether their request was granted or not. Usually, it takes two weeks, but it can be shorter.

Experience hosts pay 20% of the total sale price in commission to Airbnb. The commission is deducted at the time of payment. While the amount may seem excessive, Airbnb uses it to provide support and resources to hosts. The Experience fee is different from the standard Airbnb fee. If you rent a property and host an experience, Airbnb will charge you separately as a host and an Experience host.

Whether or not you should provide an experience depends on your background. If you're looking to boost your income and can offer a service, Airbnb Experiences might be for you. A total of 150 experiences were unveiled in New York City in 2016. It has since expanded across major cities worldwide. Airbnb has benefited because it can now offer its services in areas with limitations or restrictions on Airbnb rentals.

Chesky, the CEO of Airbnb, reported that the company has grown 12 times in size since January 2017 (GMS, 2018). Airbnb's Experiences business grew 13 times faster than its rental property business during the same period. According to reports, the Experiences division generated $1 billion for Airbnb during the second quarter of 2019.

The cost of an experience can range from $25-$150. Typically, people spend $55 each on a single activity. In 2020, Airbnb introduced its Online Experiences program, expanding the service. As of 2022, over 40,000 activities are listed in more than 1000 cities worldwide (GMS, 2018). When it comes to choosing an activity, there are several options. They include:

- Classes & Workshops
- Concerts
- Arts
- Food & Drink
- Sports
- Nature
- Music

- Entertainment
- History
- Nightlife
- Social Impact
- Health & Wellness

Experiences are not considered "passive income" but it is a nice way to increase profits. I won't go into further detail about Airbnb Experiences in this book, but it's worth exploring as you grow your business and want to increase your profits.

2

HOW TO MAKE BIG MONEY ON AIRBNB WITHOUT OWNING PROPERTY

Airbnb has a major advantage over many other platforms that let you rent out your home: flexibility. Airbnb has grown tremendously since its founding, and there are several ways to earn money from the platform. Traditionally, you can make money by buying property and renting it out or becoming a property manager. Rental arbitrage is another method used by successful entrepreneurs, and it has proven to be lucrative. Let's take a closer look at each of them.

RENT YOUR PROPERTY

The most common way to earn money from Airbnb is to buy a home and list it for rent. A home is a valuable asset but is often not used to its full potential as an income generator. Hosting guests at your home could be a practical way to earn extra income. Make sure you do your research to estimate your costs and earnings accurately.

There are many benefits to hosting your property on AirBnB. The most obvious being extra income. But many hosts use their earnings to pay off their mortgages faster. Airbnb virtually lets you live for free!

However, remember that you will need to put down a lot of money and commit to a mortgage, so if the property doesn't work out, you will have no choice but to let it go. Also, scaling is difficult unless you have a lot of money at your disposal.

Here are a few other cons of purchasing a home to start an Airbnb business.`

▷ **Initial Costs are High**

When you buy a primary residence, you can sometimes get a mortgage with a down payment as low as 5%. Vacation rental properties have different rules. Generally, you will have to pay between 20-30% of the price of your new house if you are not planning on living there. Furthermore, since you will have more obligations, your credit score requirements for a second home will likely be higher.

▷ You'll Need to Check With Your Mortgage Lender

You may be able to rent out portions of your home with some mortgage companies, but others may not allow you to do this. Contact your mortgage company and let them know what you plan to do. In the event that your existing mortgage does not permit you to short-term rent out a portion of your residence, it might be worth switching lenders or mortgages to one that does. You must notify your lender when you wish to rent out the entire house. The majority of personal mortgages assume you will live in the property full-time, so you might have to change mortgages if you plan on renting it out.

▷ Consult Your Housing Association (HOA)

Property guidelines for some properties managed by HOA's may restrict or prohibit short-term rentals. If they don't allow it, contact the Board of Directors. Airbnb might not be well known to the Board, and if you can convince them that there will be no disruption to neighbors, disturbance, or negative impact, you might be able to get them to change their minds. Some hosts have found it beneficial to pay a portion of their Airbnb rental charges to their HOA fund (increasing their rental rates to cover this), which helped them convince the Board to go along with the plan. It may also be helpful to let the Board know that your insurance covers accidents and damage to common areas.

▷ Changing Market Conditions

The real estate market can change rapidly no matter where you live. Changing trends can be influenced by changes in the general real estate market or factors specific to the area. For example, a new tourist attraction can positively affect the market. The loss of a significant employer in the area might be a negative change. This can make it more challenging to get Airbnb bookings.

▷ Additional Fees and Taxes

If you rent your house for fewer than 14 days a year, you won't have to pay taxes. If you rent your home for more than 14 days, you must file an income-tax return. You will also have to pay property, state, and local taxes. Depending on your local tax laws, you may need a business license to collect sales taxes, or you may need to collect hotel taxes separately, depending on state regulations.

▷ Surprise Bills

While renting out your property, equipment can malfunction or stop working. If this happens, you will be responsible for covering the repair costs. No one is prepared for a malfunctioning washing machine or a burst water pipe. Setting aside 1% of the purchase price for maintenance every year is advisable.

▷ **Unexpected events**

Imagine your property is located in a city where the value drops suddenly when it is struck by a tornado or mentioned negatively in the media? If you fall ill, what will happen to your property? Although you can't predict when these things will occur, you can prepare for them. It's important to determine whether you can afford to pay your mortgage if Airbnb rentals decline or stop altogether. Whenever you plan to purchase a home to rent on Airbnb, it is essential to keep an eye on the unforeseen and to make sure your plans include enough wiggle room to accommodate any unforeseen circumstances.

BECOME AN AIRBNB PROPERTY MANAGER (AKA A CO-HOST)

Another way to make money on Airbnb is to become a co-host. Managing an Airbnb property can be time consuming. Many hosts decide to hire a co-host to manage their properties and guests. Often, they are a family member, an acquaintance, a close friend, or an experienced person the host has hired.

This method involves collaborating with a property owner or several property owners and taking on the role of their property manager. If you are looking for property owners, you can contact them through rental listing sites or websites like Craigslist. Ask them if they are comfortable putting their properties on Airbnb (you manage the listing, they get cash: it's a win-win situation).

Prepare a resumé that shows potential partners that you have the experience and expertise needed to manage short-term rental properties on Airbnb. If you have experience managing listings, you should mention which listings you have handled and describe your responsibilities in detail.

In the event that you are hired, the Airbnb account-owner will add you to the listing. Once you accept the co-host invitation, you will become an Airbnb co-host. You can manage the listing directly from your Airbnb co-host account.

Co-hosts are required to agree to the Terms of Service. However, owners and co-hosts are free to negotiate their own terms. All agreements and guidelines should be clearly spelled out.

Owners and co-hosts should clearly define hosting duties and be specific about what each person does, determine how much each earns, and make reimbursement arrangements. You can negotiate your fee and get up to 30% of the listing value depending on the service you provide

There is the option to use or modify a pre-written Airbnb co-host contract. Or you can hire an attorney to draft the contract for you. Depending on your agreement, you may choose to perform a portion of the services or take on the entire process.

One of the best things about this method is that it does not require a large investment up front; meaning that anyone can start and successfully run an Airbnb business. This method also allows you to save the funds you need to start your Airbnb rental business. Once you've found the right partner, this is much easier to scale than buying a rental property.

The downside is that you won't make as much money as you would if you owned the property and you'll probably have to do the bulk of the work to ensure the listing is profitable.

RENTAL ARBITRAGE

The third option, and the subject matter of this book, is rental arbitrage. You will rent a house and advertise it on Airbnb (legally). Through this method, you will see your ROI in just nine days.

Arbitrage is a business model in which you purchase something at a low price in one market and then sell it in another market for a higher price. Arbitrage is a game of spotting these potential profits by doing simple math. Every business in the world is engaged in some kind of arbitrage. For example, when you buy peanut butter from a grocery store and pay $5 for the jar, you're paying a higher price than the grocery store paid for that jar of peanut butter. This is peanut butter arbitrage.

So how does this work with Airbnb?

With Airbnb arbitrage you can earn supplemental income or even a stable full-time salary. You don't need to own a property to host guests on Airbnb. Sublease agreements can be arranged to rent out the property.

Over the past few years, rental arbitrage has become increasingly popular, especially as more people become aware of the opportunity Airbnb provides. Arbitrage is about finding discrepancies in a market and taking advantage of them. Almost every market has weaknesses and inefficiencies you can take advantage of and make a good living from. Airbnb has helped many savvy entrepreneurs generate substantial income each month, and they do it without owning a single property. They identify specific weaknesses in the property market and take advantage of them. The process is simple; with a bit of patience and solid research abilities, you can start your Airbnb arbitrage business.

Let me give you a simple example. Imagine finding a beautiful apartment in a desirable neighborhood for $1,500 a month. You then checked Airbnb in the same area and discovered that renting a similar apartment costs $100 a day. The math is simple. If you were to rent out that apartment for 30 consecutive days, it would be $100 x 30 = $3,000. This means you would earn $1,500. The reality is you won't lease out your property for the whole 30 days since there will be times when there are no guests (cleaning, etc.). If the apartment is rented for 20 days out of 30, you will still earn $500 per month.

Property owners value their property and subletting their property must be beneficial to them as well. If you don't present your business professionally, the owner may not consider you for a lease. Your goal is to present a profitable plan. Tell them how much potential their property holds and how Airbnb can help them earn more money. It may be necessary to modify the rental agreement and perhaps offer them a better price for the property than they are currently getting. However, only take action if you are confident that the numbers support your proposal.

People look for temporary housing for a variety of reasons. Hotels are a popular choice. However, most people dislike the restrictions, rules, and requirements that make staying in a hotel uncomfortable. This is where Airbnb comes in. Renting an Airbnb apartment is a better choice when looking for a "home away from home" experience. With rental arbitrage, you can start making money in this growing market right away.

PROPERTY MANAGEMENT VS. RENTAL ARBITRAGE

Rental arbitrage may seem similar to property management. However, they are not quite the same. As a landlord, the idea of you renting their property as a short-term rental might be nerve-racking. However, there are a number of convincing reasons why they would prefer you over a property management company.

By renting their property to you, they avoid the cost and responsibilities of a property manager since you eliminate both of these issues. Instead of charging any fees, you pay the landlord a steady, consistent payment as if you were renting, and you earn your income from the rental spread. The spread is the difference between the amount you receive and the amount you spend. Rent is the money you spend, and profits from your Airbnb rentals are the money you receive. Rental arbitrage is favored over property management by investors because they don't have to pay you, and you do most of the work.

The main disadvantage of hiring a property manager is the financial burden. Property managers understand passive income is what investors desire most. Therefore, their prices are based on the profit the investor makes each month, requiring a month's rent to cover vacancies and a percentage of the profit afterward. A major disadvantage of hiring a property manager is the cost! Typically, landlords cannot afford such a high fee, so they are left to manage their rental properties independently. They then must spend a lot of time on property management, typically lack the skills to do proper research, promotion, or administration. You're removing this headache for property owners!

CAN'T PROPERTY OWNERS DO THIS THEMSELVES?

If I can do it, anyone can do it. Why don't real estate investors take advantage of this strategy, given how profitable it is? A lot of them do. There are a lot of investors who invest in short-term rentals. However, there are two key reasons why most investors don't do this on their own. Most property owners start by trying to earn additional revenue from their properties. Tenant turnover is much higher, and management is much more complicated. Due to the perceived time commitment, many landlords are reluctant to take on this additional workload. However, it's not as difficult as they think.

HOW MUCH DOES IT COST TO START AN AIRBNB ARBITRAGE BUSINESS?

You can expect to pay at least $3,000 to $15,000. This includes your lease payments, fixtures and decorations, bedding and kitchenware, and listing photography. The most appealing aspect of rental arbitrage is that you do not have to purchase any assets. Therefore, you won't have to save up a lot of money for a down payment. You will also not have to pay for costly property upkeep. Even though it's not as expensive as buying a house, there are still some upfront expenses.

I spent approximately $5,000 on my first rental arbitrage property. Within two months, I recouped that initial cost.

Rental Security Deposits

Committing to a long-term rental agreement is one of the first things you'll need to budget for. Here are a few upfront costs to consider:

- Rent for the first month
- Payment for last month's rent
- Security deposit

BENEFITS OF AIRBNB ARBITRAGE

Airbnb and other short-term rental services are growing rapidly worldwide. You will gain valuable experience by hosting on Airbnb. You will learn about financial management, marketing, and customer service. Among other things, Airbnb investing will help you improve your investment skills. The world is your oyster. The following are a few benefits of doing rental arbitrage on Airbnb.

You Can Use Automated Systems to Run Your Business

Airbnb hosts can use several tools to manage their properties more efficiently, especially if they have multiple properties. In addition to hiring staff, such as housekeepers and property supervisors, hosts must also maintain positive guest relations. Most hosts prefer to build these relationships independently rather than relying on their staff. However, there are software programs designed explicitly for Airbnb that can make reservations for you, create schedules for your employees, and help you stay organized. In addition, you can assess the reviews that you receive quickly and make any adjustments to your system if needed.

You Can Have Properties Across the Country

You can rent Airbnbs across the country, and manage them all using your staff, Airbnb's software, and by implementing the same systems across the board. Your business can then be leveraged to earn a substantial income. By building your own Airbnb empire, you will earn passive income and have "vacation" properties all over the country.

Expand Into Other Areas in Real Estate

Airbnb might be your first business venture, but you're probably interested in expanding into other areas. For example, you might flip houses and rent them out as Airbnbs or sell them for income. As an Airbnb host, you can develop several skills that you cannot learn in other real estate fields. This can benefit you in many ways, including feeling more confident to try new things.

Getting to Know People From Around the World

Your guests will come from all over the world. As a host, you will meet people from all walks of life who will be eager to share their experiences. You will gain a deeper understanding of cultures other than your own and learn a new way of thinking. You will learn more than you ever imagined. You might even receive repeat business! Providing excellent service to your guests will make them more appreciative of you.

Potential Earnings

You will be rewarded handsomely if you are careful about managing your property and choose an excellent location. You may feel financially overwhelmed when you first launch your Airbnb business. The more effort you put into marketing, operations, and customer service; the more successful your rental will be. The income from Airbnb rentals varies. Some people earn only $500 a month, while others earn close to $10,000. The average host makes around $900 per month (Leasca, 2017). It is important to realize that your earnings will fluctuate from month to month. Depending on the location of your property, you may have more visitors during the warm months of June, July, and August. You will therefore earn more money during these months.

Before you start bringing in revenue from your rental arbitrage business, you need to convince the landlord to cooperate. Your landlord must be aware of and approve of you subletting their residence. You cannot sublet without their permission. In the next chapter, we'll go into details around how to convince any landlord to do business with you.

AIRBNB ARBITRAGE: IS IT RIGHT FOR YOU?

Airbnb Arbitrage is not for the faint of heart. Instead of focusing on the money, think about whether hosting is right for you. Nevertheless, it can be a lucrative business for anyone, and because it is a cost-effective method, there is a low barrier to entry. You won't be charged to list on Airbnb, and you can cover ongoing expenses with your earnings.

Airbnb arbitrage offers more than just financial rewards. You can set your own schedule and work at your own pace. It can be run full-time, part-time, or even on the side.

You can run an Airbnb arbitrage business while working a day job, traveling the world, or raising a family. With this method, you'll spend the least amount of money upfront to earn the maximum profit (and fast).

3

THE SIMPLE STEPS TO MAKE MONEY ON AIRBNB WITHOUT OWNING A PROPERTY

We briefly discussed the theory of rental arbitrage in the last chapter, and now we will discuss how this method can be used to generate income. Airbnb rental arbitrage is the practice of renting out properties to sublet them on Airbnb. Even though it may seem easy and appealing, there are still legal issues to consider before deciding to make money through Airbnb arbitrage.

There is always a need for short-term housing. Hotels can be very pricey in large cities and tourist areas. Airbnb fills a market gap by offering more affordable accommodations. Previously, you needed a lot of money to purchase a rental property and list it on Airbnb. Now you can earn a lot of money by listing a rental on Airbnb with a price higher than the property's rental rate.

Nevertheless, the property must still be less than a person would pay for a similar room in a nearby hotel. The steps involved in listing your property and taking advantage of this opportunity will require some effort, but the process is pretty straightforward. Let's look at a brief example of how a rental can be used to generate a lot of revenue without a lot of upfront investment.

To start an Airbnb business the traditional way, you must first purchase a property. If you were buying a $400,000 home, 25% would be required for a down payment and closing costs. Before you can even consider getting a mortgage, you'd need at least $100,000. You are then responsible for paying your mortgage, taxes, liability, and maintenance.

You can enter the market much more cheaply and scale up much faster if you rent out rental properties. To illustrate, here are the numbers:

For $1,500 per month, you rent a furnished apartment. A $1,500 security-deposit is also required, bringing your total start-up cost to $3,000. You decide to list the property on Airbnb for $150 per night. After 20 nights, you've made back your investment. As a bonus, you will generate a profit in your first month.

Before you decide to provide Airbnb accommodations, you should conduct thorough market research. First, you need to determine which areas are best for you. A successful vacation rental business depends on finding a property in a desirable neighborhood. Maintaining the property will be difficult without a steady stream of rental income. If you're still unsure about which cities are worth your attention, take a closer look at the list of the top tourist cities in the country. Generally, large cities with plenty of tourist attractions are more appealing to travelers. Choose a property that is close to major attractions and services (such as a metro station or grocery store). It may seem like a good idea to rent a property on the city's outskirts because of the low monthly cost, but you'll likely have a hard time renting it out.

A property near a beach will usually have a high nightly rate. Nevertheless, before starting your Airbnb business, check out the rental rates of similar properties in the surrounding area. Based on the average vacancy rate and the costs involved, you can determine your income and choose the best option for you.

Almost everyone wonders if this strategy is legal. Fortunately, it is! However, it hinges on the following two factors.

LOCAL LAWS AND REGULATIONS

An important aspect to consider when earning money through rental arbitrage is local laws and regulations. Recently, many cities have imposed stricter rules and restrictions around short-term rentals. You may be able to rent out your home legally, but there may be restrictions on the number of nights you can rent out. Is it possible to make a significant profit by renting out your property, for example, for 90 days only? This is definitely something to consider if you want to avoid going into debt.

Most hotel owners and operators dislike Airbnb. Since Airbnb became popular in 2008, a growing number of people are staying at Airbnbs rather than hotels. As a result, hotels in some areas are losing guests at an alarming rate. Many hotels are aware of the decline of their business, which they attribute to Airbnb. Some hotels have taken legal action to prevent Airbnbs from operating, and many business owners are at risk because of these restrictions. When establishing a business location, it is important to establish a relationship with the local, county, and state authorities. Make sure you adhere to all regulations, rules, and restrictions in your location. Failure to do so could result in charges or a fine. If you do not follow all the regulations, you may be forced to close your Airbnb. In this scenario, your rental property would be losing money, but you would still have to pay your bills and fines. Check your city's laws regarding short-term rentals to ensure that you are following the law. Airbnb itself is also an excellent resource for determining whether short-term rentals are legal by doing a quick search for other listings in your prospective location.

CONFIRM WITH LANDLORD

To ensure that short-term rentals are legal, you should also check with your landlord or another vacation rental website. You also must obtain permissions to sublet your property from your landlord prior to starting operations.

I rented before buying my own house. Before moving out, I thought about how to cover up any blunders that might have happened. When something was damaged, I didn't fix it; I just assumed the property owner wouldn't notice. However, after buying my first home, I changed my mind. Now, if I break something, I feel stung. If something is damaged, I am responsible. My house is a part of me, and I feel hurt when it is neglected. Your landlord probably feels the same way. They probably worked hard to save for the down payment, buy it, and maintain it. When something breaks, they have to fix it. The house is their source of income and damaged items reduce their profits. The condition of their air conditioner, walls, and floors will affect their profitability.

Understanding a landlord's mindset is essential to developing a partnership. You will likely encounter questions and concerns when you speak with them. You must convince them that you can protect their investment and ensure that you have their best interests at heart (protecting their property while profiting). When you speak with a property owner, they will be intrigued by what you have to say. Ultimately, property owners want truly passive income from their investments.

I know from my own experience that property management is not passive, especially if it's a one-person operation. They will have questions for you. Generally, homeowners will want to know that you're taking care of their home with a high level of care. You may also be asked about your business model. They are business people who know that a business cannot exist if it is not profitable. Conversations with landlords may seem awkward initially, but it gets easier once you secure a deal. The landlords want your help, so it's not as hard as it may seem. Every investor wants a quick profit without doing much work. All that's left is to convince them that their dream can come true.

It is possible that you will be rejected, so you need to be prepared for that outcome. If a landlord does reject your proposal and refuses to participate in the deal, then do your best to find out why that's the case. You should ask them questions and address them until you understand their concerns. You may be able to pay more than the typical rent or put down a larger deposit if it is a financial problem. Ultimately, landlords may refuse to rent to you, which is okay. There is no point in burning bridges with potential landlords; instead, make sure they know you are available to talk to them if their decision changes. In real estate, numbers are crucial. It may take 50 landlords before the first one agrees. Keep trying. Send texts, emails, and phone calls as often as you can. If you find a landlord willing to work with you, ensure you treat them well. Providing excellent service will make you a successful marketer, and when you provide excellent service, your investor will tell their friends.

It is crucial to have a clear, upfront, and mutually agreed upon contract to ensure you and your landlord are being honest and open with each other. To avoid future surprises, confirm the agreement is included in the lease. Don't worry; I'll provide scripting for how to address landlords' four most common concerns in the next section.

In the remainder of this book, I'll walk you through how to get a positive ROI in your Airbnb business in just 9 days without owning any property. In this Step-by-step guide to starting your Airbnb business, we will cover the following topics:

DECIDE WHERE TO LAUNCH YOUR BUSINESS (1 DAY)

One of the most common mistakes entrepreneurs make when starting an Airbnb venture is not understanding their competitors and the market they are in. Making a blind decision could cost you dearly and destroy any chance you have of success.

MAKE SURE SHORT-TERM RENTALS ARE ALLOWED IN THE AREA AND UNDERSTAND THE LOCAL RENTS (1 DAY)

Regulations can negatively affect businesses, especially if they are ignored. You may lose your home or, worse yet, your investment.

FIND OUT WHAT SHORT-TERM RENTALS TYPICALLY COST (1/3 DAY)

It is impossible to fight when you cannot see. You must therefore know your opponent's strengths and weaknesses. This is easily done by searching listings currently on Airbnb to get an idea of the going rates. By doing so, you will better understand the market, the area, and the quality of available rentals.

UNDERSTANDING THE VACANCY RATE FOR SHORT-TERM RENTALS IN YOUR AREA (1/3 DAY)

You will learn how to determine the general vacancy rate in your area. Be prepared to deal with market conditions that are constantly changing and that anything can happen at any time. Because of this, the demand for housing in your chosen neighborhood may also fluctuate from month to month without warning, so you should prepare in order to protect yourself from sudden changes in the economy.

UNDERSTAND WHAT MIGHT ATTRACT VISITORS TO THE AREA, SO YOU KNOW WHO YOUR GUESTS WILL BE (1/3 DAY)

It is essential to understand the mindset of your guests. What factors do they consider when deciding whether to book a home? Airbnb searches are based on these factors. Airbnb will take into account how often guests book after seeing your property. Results that show up in searches are successful if people click on them. A sign that people are interested in learning more about the listing.

FIND THE RIGHT PROPERTY AND GET PERMISSION FROM THE OWNER TO LIST IT ON AIRBNB (1 DAY)

You cannot start an Airbnb business on your landlord's property unless they approve. Some people rent out their properties on Airbnb behind their landlords' backs, but this is a flawed strategy because if something goes wrong, it increases the risk of the business failing.

MAKE SURE YOU HAVE THE CASH UP-FRONT TO MEET THE LEASE REQUIREMENTS (0 DAYS)

Before investing in your business, you need to estimate how much it will cost. A property's price is determined by a combination of factors. You need to consider things like rent, insurance, decor, utilities, and other miscellaneous expenses. This is simple once you've found the right property - I will give you the formula.

GET YOUR MANAGEMENT PLAN IN ORDER AND PREPARE THE PROPERTY FOR GUESTS (3 DAYS)

Today, automation plays a significant role in our lives, making life easier for our guests and us. You no longer need to spend your time on tedious tasks since they can be automated and executed remotely, as required. Automating your Airbnb rentals can help you stay ahead of the competition in the property management industry.

CREATE YOUR LISTING, DRIVE TRAFFIC TO THAT LISTING, & SCALE! (2 DAYS)

Even though pictures can reveal a lot about a house, the description is equally as important. The description addresses several things that a picture cannot. Be sure to provide your guests with accurate and detailed information. Airbnb has created a lot of growth opportunities, and people are making considerable money from it. Several have even left their 9-5 jobs to concentrate on growing their Airbnb business. You can do the same!

4

FINDING & SECURING THE RIGHT PROPERTY TO LIST ON AIRBNB

I t's important to not overthink this. Finding the right property is a breeze and there are tools that can help you. You should be able to complete this entire step in no more than four days, including signing the lease with the landlord.

DECIDE ON A GOOD LOCATION

Airbnb is a great way to invest in properties, but you must do your research. In this chapter, I will discuss topics like the best location for investing in property with Airbnb, setting up optimal rental rates, and more. You will get a step-by-step guide for finding houses, renting them, and obtaining a license to host them on Airbnb.

The first step is determining which areas will provide the greatest return on investment. Location, location, location! Investing in the right place is crucial to success. Location affects rental rates, vacancy rates, expenditures, and cash flow, but there are other factors to consider as well.

Even though local travel demand greatly influences the profitability of your listing, you can still profit as a host if you live outside of the most popular travel areas. Airbnb properties are best to invest in if they are located in cities with many tourist attractions that bring a steady stream of visitors or in areas with a lot of business activity. However, smaller locations should not be overlooked, especially if they have seasonal customers, are more affordable, and have fewer competitors. AIRDNA reports that Santa Rosa Beach, FL is the most profitable city for Airbnb, with an average revenue per available rental of $119,116 (Air-DNA, 2019).

The desired area should be centrally located to the city's main attractions with easy access to amenities (grocery stores, restaurants) and public transit (buses, trains). Do not restrict your search to your immediate neighborhood. Explore other regions, states, and even countries. If you travel frequently, keep an eye out for good deals.

BECOME FAMILIAR WITH LOCAL LAWS

Each city governs Airbnb differently, and the law is constantly changing. When starting your Airbnb business, be aware of and educated about the local laws in your town.

Suppose you are aware of the short-term rental laws in your city. In that case, whether they are already in place or are about to be implemented, you can avoid expensive penalties from city officials and be aware of how they may affect your earnings. Several cities worldwide have enacted or are considering harsher penalties for operators of illegal short-term rentals. In order to avoid heavy fines, you are encouraged to research local short-term rental laws before renting out your property.

LOCAL LAWS AND YOUR PROFITABILITY

Getting a License or Permit

To manage an Airbnb listing properly in your city, you might need to apply for and pay for a permit or license. Additionally, some cities only allow short-term rentals in certain areas and limit the number of permits that can be issued.

Heavy Fines

You could face heavy penalties if you list an illegal property without the appropriate license or permit. In 2022, an individual from Singapore was fined $845,000 for illegally renting out short-term apartments on Airbnb. In 2019, a tenant in London who sublet his own home through Airbnb was evicted and fined a record amount of $100,000 (BBC News, 2019).

Profitability

Airbnb hosting laws may drastically decrease your income. Suppose your property can only be used as a short-term rental for 90 days. If so, you need to decide whether that is long enough to make Airbnb hosting worthwhile.

If you Google "Airbnb law (your city name)," you will find results for many localities that have passed or are working on enacting short-term rental laws.

CHOOSING THE RIGHT PROPERTY TO LEASE

First-time investors can benefit from renting out Airbnb properties at a reasonable price. When you do a little research, you'll find many interesting properties, such as villas and houses with pools, that you might not be able to afford. You don't need to worry; plenty of properties are available that are perfect for your needs. Keep in mind that not everyone wants to stay in a fancy house in an exotic location. Typical Airbnb guests are looking for a peaceful place to relax for a few days with their loved ones or, if they are a business traveler, a place close to their office at a reasonable price, rather than a beautiful home.

Furthermore, the more expensive the property is, the greater the investment and the greater the risk. When looking at Airbnb properties, you should not only consider what type of property you want, but what kind of guests you will be hosting based on the location. If the location is a draw for honeymooners, you should consider the types of properties that will suit their needs; if the location is more suited for families or people seeking an authentic way to connect with nature through experiential travel, then find a space that meets those needs.

CHECK OUT AIRBNB TO SEE HOW MUCH OTHER LISTINGS IN THE AREA ARE GOING FOR

If you want to get the best rental price for your space, you should research other nearby properties. Increasing your rate too much might result in fewer bookings, but decreasing your rate and charging too little might mean that you miss out on potential profits. Once you have done your homework and are sure you have the best rate, you can then adjust as the number of bookings increase or decrease based on the vacancy level in the area and the time of year. Make sure your listing price is always current, or you may not rent your space at the best price. If you are new to listing properties, there are tools to assist with price calculation, but you should also conduct independent research.

UNDERSTAND THE BUDGET NEEDED FOR THE LEASE AND MAKE SURE IT FITS YOUR NEEDS

Getting a return on investment is heavily influenced by your business objectives. So, by determining the weighted average price in the area, you can better assess your chances of profitability.

Here is the formula (iGMS, 2020):

1. Calculate the Standard Daily Rental Cost for Weekdays and Weekends in Your Location.

Airbnb listings provide this information directly. Find similar properties near you and note down the weekend and weekday costs for each. Use a spreadsheet to keep track.

2. Determining the Weighted Average Airbnb Price for all Properties

Weighted Average Airbnb Price = ((Weekday Average Airbnb Rate * 5) + (Weekend Average Airbnb Rate * 2)) / 7

If the average Airbnb rate is $100 during the week and $200 during the weekend, then the weighted average Airbnb rate would be $128, since (($100 * 5) + ($200 * 2)) / 7 = $128.

3. Estimate the Price of Your Property Maintenance Costs Daily

Divide the total amount you spend on the property each month by 30 to determine how much you spend each day.

If your monthly property expenses (including rent and any fees) total $1,500, you will incur a daily expense of $50.

4. Calculate the Weighted Average Airbnb by Dividing it by the Cost of Your Property per day

The final ratio is calculated by dividing the weighted average price by the daily property price. It will help you determine how many days per month you'll need to rent your property to make a profit.

In this example, the final ratio is $128/$50 = 2.56.

With this ratio, you won't need to lease your property for the majority of the month to make a profit. However, if the final ratio is less than 1, then your property will not be profitable because you're spending more in expenses than you could possible bring in via rental income.

Let's say the weighted average Airbnb price is $48, and you still spend $50 per day on property expenses. That gives you a total percentage of 0.96 ($48/$67), which means you would not be able to generate a return within a month.

Arbitrage should be used on properties with a Final Ratio of 2.0 or higher to achieve the best results. If you aim for a higher Final Ratio, you can make adjustments as you go. This will ensure that you make a profit each month from your property.

TAKE THE TIME TO SEARCH THOROUGHLY

The internet is the first place most people go when they start their search. Zillow is a popular website for searching and finding rental properties. If you visit Zillow or another listing website, you may be able to speak directly with the homeowner, but a realtor or property manager is valuable too. When starting your

Airbnb business, you should contact agents with experience renting out properties. You might gain their support by sounding credible and explaining what you are trying to accomplish, which could prove very beneficial.

Craigslist is another option. You can find property managers and other professionals who assist renters in finding housing. Get in touch with them. Do not be afraid to explore different avenues. Get in touch with people, tell them what you want, and together you might be able to accomplish something. There are also meetups where you can meet people and connect with people who may be able to help you.

Finding a place to rent requires a lot of creativity, and you must always be on the lookout. You can search Zillow and Craigslist, contact Realtors, attend local meetup groups, and start making acquaintances.

A property owner might list their rental online, searching for a reliable renter to take care of their property. Keep hunting for those listings. They are out there. When you help others solve their problems and generate income, they are more likely to offer you opportunities to increase your income, which will help your business thrive.

TOOLS FOR YOUR AIRBNB INVESTMENT PROPERTY

You don't have to struggle to find the perfect property! There are some shortcuts you can take in the form of tools that will streamline your research. For you to find your ideal rental property that offers the best accommodation and rent, you must have a detailed understanding of the market, including the major factors that influence rental rates and property prices. Below, I detail out a few tools that can help you with this.

Mashvisor

Mashvisor is an excellent resource for investors looking for properties. Mashvisor helps investors identify properties that are likely to generate significant returns in both the long-term and short-term rental markets.

Mashvisor is a web-based tool that helps real estate investors find the right investment. It provides real estate information and the necessary resources to make an informed decision. Mashvisor can help you with:

- Developing a strategy to maximize rental income
- Become familiar with the specifics of the market and monitor its development

- Identify investment opportunities

The LITE plan will give you the tools you need for $17.99/month.

AirDNA

AirDNA provides its users with various tools to assist them in finding lucrative investment properties. Platform users can access competitive data, customized reports, and a dashboard that displays data from more than 10 million rental properties in 120,000 markets around the world. You can use this tool to identify and evaluate trends in the short-term rental market, combining historical and future data to increase profits. Under its umbrella are two powerful products (MarketMinder, and Rentalizer).

MarketMinder

MarketMinder lets you compare your rental property with other homes in the area and see the future demand as rates are set in real-time.

Investors can use MarketMinder to:

- Search for investment opportunities
- Evaluate future demand against comparables in the area
- Set prices intelligently and correctly

- Develop a profitable listing portfolio

Rentalizer

Rentalizer is an evaluation tool for estimating Airbnb income potential when turning a house into a rental. AirDNA does not offer a search function for properties. Therefore, you should already know the address of the place you want to search, or you can find it on another platform.

Investors can use Rentalizer to:

- Check out other hosts in their area to see how their rental home compares
- To estimate the possible income of a rental home

HOW TO PITCH LANDLORDS

Once you've shortlisted a few properties, negotiating with your landlord can be one of the most intimidating parts of the process. It can bring up a lot of stress and worry, particularly when you don't have a rapport with a landlord. To help combat those feelings, you can use this sample script to contact prospective landlords.

Sample Script

"(Landlord), Thank you for showing your property. It's perfect, and I'm ready to sign the lease agreement right now. Let me tell you what sets me apart from the average tenant, and we can decide if we are a good match. I may not be a good fit for you, but let me show you what I can do to be your best tenant, and together we can see if we can make it work."

The landlord can either decline or ask for more information. Let's assume they want more information.

- You: "I'd like to lease your home for a year. As a good tenant, I will pay you promptly and take good care of your property. If you agree, I would like to rent the property to others needing short-term housing. Honestly, I wouldn't live in the property since that's how I run my business, but I can help you maximize the profitability of your property."
- Property owner: "Can you explain? Is it Airbnb? You are interested in subletting the property?"

Until you fully explain your business plan, you should avoid discussing Airbnb. If they aren't comfortable with Airbnb, you can suggest other sites they may find more suitable.

- You: "First, I will offer guests the opportunity to stay at the property for two or three nights during their visit to the city. This is my role. Furthermore, I assist property owners in avoiding tenants who do not pay their rent on time. Whenever I have guests over, I ensure the property is well maintained, have liability insurance for the property, and keep up with any minor maintenance issues. So, you can kick back and earn money. If you're open to working with me, I can sign the lease as soon as possible."

Remember, selling is an art; you will learn what works and what landlords are most interested in as you go.

Be aware that there are many things to consider before you begin negotiating with landlords. Do not argue or get combative. You are not the only one concerned – the landlord will also be anxious. A landlord might be excited and take action immediately. If the landlord is unsure about your plan, invite them to a meeting and explain your research and strategy. Make yourself available for any questions, comments, and concerns they may have. Be friendly and nod your head when they speak. You should also give them some time to digest what you are saying. Focus more on listening than talking. The landlord may ask questions you didn't anticipate. If you are a first-time renter, your property manager may give you some advice and tips to help you.

Here are tips for pitching landlords and responding to their most common concerns.

Landlords are Worried About Turnover Costs...but You Will Never Move out

"I intend to sign a one-year lease. I am committed to making money, which is why I will extend and renew my lease as soon as possible. Turnover is probably your biggest expense, so securing me as a tenant will take your property to the next level. We will work together to create a smooth experience and I will be a consistent tenant for a long time."

Short-Term Renters Mean More Wear and Tear...

"My short-term rentals are immaculately maintained because renters expect it. You receive monthly payments regardless of how much I earn. For my business to be profitable, I must keep people coming back. I clean after each short-term rental. A negative review would be left if the property smelled of smoke or pets, appeared dirty, contained mold, or was damaged. Negative reviews cost me money, so I avoid them as much as possible, which means that I will keep your property in incredible condition. I am passionate about my business and want to ensure you are happy."

Will You Pay My Rent on Time?

"Since I run a successful business, I can pay my rent on time. The number of people renting short-term apartments has increased, and I've thoroughly researched this area to ensure that we will stay busy. This means that you will always be paid on time."

Why Should I Trust You and not Do it Myself...

"Airbnb is fairly straightforward, but promoting and making profits on Airbnb is labor-intensive and a skill. You would need to decorate the house, take photos, write the listing, and be available to answer potential guests' questions. It will take a lot of work! Let me handle it! I will handle all of the details and maintain the entire property. Then you can sit back and watch the money roll in."

Rental arbitrage is a lucrative business, not just for tenants but also for landlords. Renting out your property to another party can be risky for landlords, but it can also be very beneficial. And if you build the right relationships with landlords, then your business will grow very quickly!

LEASE AGREEMENT AND INSURANCE

Once you have received the landlord's approval, you can begin working on your company. However, you should ensure the rental agreement states that you are allowed to rent the property short-term. Since temporary-housing regulations can change anytime, you should consult an attorney to ensure you comply with your landlord and business.

Airbnb provides a $1 million host protection policy, which protects you as a business owner and helps cover any losses on your property during a guest stay. Airbnb's policy is excellent since it provides third-party coverage for damage guests may cause for up to $1 million. As an added safeguard, Airbnb's host protection policy is effective. However, it should not be relied on exclusively.

You should protect yourself against the possibility of liability since you don't want to be in a position where you are not covered in case of an unfortunate event. Despite Airbnb's protection, you should use multiple methods to protect yourself and your belongings.

Property insurance protects you from loss caused by an event on your property. You need to take steps to reduce or prevent damage to property or injury to individuals. A backup plan is essential in case anything goes wrong.

You may be responsible for any problems or losses if you don't obtain the proper liability coverage designed for short-term accommodations. The most important thing is to make sure you are insured.

Make sure you are fully aware of your insurance policy. I recommend purchasing a liability insurance policy to cover any damage to your property. Make sure your policy covers the property if it is rented out for a short period of time. Now, if a guest damages your property, you have three options:

- Your guest's security deposit is your first line of defense.
- Your second line of defense is Airbnb's liability policy.
- The third line of defense is your own personal insurance.

You can rest assured that your property is protected since you have insurance coverage covering all types of damage. All three are necessary to guarantee your protection. You will almost certainly be prepared for the worst-case scenario.

BONUS: FIVE BEST CITIES FOR RENTAL ARBITRAGE

To kick-start your research, here are the most popular U.S cities for rental arbitrage. Note that I do recommend renting a property near you when you're getting started. Once you've mastered the basics, you might want to venture to one of these cities.

1. Oklahoma City, OK
2. St. Paul, MN
3. Annapolis, MD
4. Nashville, TN
5. North Las Vegas, NV

(Zaragoza, 2021)

Don't overthink this. There are many opportunities. You just have to find them and decide. You choose the price point, so even a small budget will work!

GETTING YOUR PROPERTY READY FOR GUESTS (AND PROFITS)

You'll dedicate the next three days to getting your rental ready - if you opted for a furnished property, you'll focus on the final touches to make it feel like a home. Let's look at how you can set up your Airbnb so that your guests are pleased. Remember, you only get one chance at a first impression! Be patient. Before opening your space to paying guests, here are some things to consider in order to maximize your earnings

WHY DO GUESTS CHOOSE AIRBNB?

Airbnb guests expect different things than hotel guests. In order to create an Airbnb experience that guests will appreciate, it's first important to understand why people choose Airbnb instead of a hotel. Here are five of the most popular reasons.

Live Like a local

Renting an Airbnb property allows guests to experience life like a local, discover a new city, and learn about local culture. They can dine at quaint restaurants, go off the beaten path, and mingle with locals. Why settle for a typical hotel stay when you can have a more intimate and unique experience?

Amenities

The major difference between Airbnbs and traditional hotels is that Airbnbs are seen as a refuge, a place to escape. It must be more than just a place to sleep; in many cases, it should have some bells and whistles in the backyard. A grill should be available for grilling, and lounge chairs and outdoor games can enhance the experience.

Personal Interaction With the Owner

It is crucial that guests can communicate with you. That is what separates Airbnb hosts from hotel chains. The latter seems less personal. Guests can contact you through Airbnb, but you should also include a telephone number and an email address in case they need to reach you immediately. Before they arrive, send them a friendly pre-check-in email with directions, and follow up after they arrive to ensure everything went well.

Check-in and Check-out Flexibility

Getting the right arrival and departure times can be tricky. Travelers are on the move 24/7, so make sure your arrival and departure times are not only reasonable but also flexible. If you allow guests to change even 3 hours before their arrival, it can significantly affect whether or not they choose to book with you.

Budget-Conscious

Budget-friendly hotel rooms are definitely available. Usually, they are basic and functional. The price is affordable if guests are only staying for a night or two. If they stay for an extended period, then Airbnb is probably the better choice. Airbnbs are available almost everywhere at a reasonable price, there are no tipping requirements, and having a kitchen saves you a lot of money on food.

CLEANING: DON'T MISS A SPOT

The number one complaint from guests is that a property is not clean. A guest who complains about the cleanliness of your apartment will negatively affect your earnings. Most people will leave a bad review if they notice a possible sanitary problem. This will definitely affect the number of bookings you receive and the profit that you earn. When an apartment is clean, fresh, and free of mold, it will appear more spacious, smell better, and look more inviting. While friends may be satisfied with a free room, paying customers deserve more. A light cleaning every now and then is not enough. Deep clean your guest rooms and the areas where guests will spend time in your home.

When you get access to your space, start by checking the ceiling, the heating system, the lighting, and the shelves above the closet. Dust underneath dressers and mattresses, and clean the walls, photos, and baseboards. I once stayed in a hotel that appeared clean until a pen fell, and it ended up under the table. When I went to look for it, I was horrified by the cobwebs and dust.

Particular attention should be paid to the bathroom, especially the shower and toilet.

Clean the windows inside and outside, and make sure your blinds are working properly. Invest in professional cleaning services for the carpet, furnishings, cushions, and draperies.

There are several inexpensive methods to remove dirt and hard-to-remove marks using items you already own or can get for a reasonable price. Broom balls can be used to remove scratches on painted surfaces. Paint can be removed from surfaces by putting them under a hair dryer set to a warm temperature and wiping them with a cloth. You can also use this method to remove difficult stickers from household items and devices. Mayonnaise can be used to remove watermarks from wooden furniture.

You can remove the visible imprints left by furniture legs from fabrics and rugs. You can remove them by placing a damp cotton cloth and steaming iron over them. Stains on furniture and mattresses can be removed by wiping them with a mixture of white vinegar, baking soda, and dishwashing liquid, then wiping them with a clean cloth and allowing them to air dry. Stain pens can be used to remove spots that are not too large.

Mix one part vinegar with two parts liquid to clean glass. You can clean window tracks by sprinkling baking soda over them, followed by white vinegar. Let the mixture stand for 30 minutes. You can dissolve the oil and grime on the track by brushing it with a toothbrush and then wiping it. Wrap the cloth with a knife or something sharp to clean the borders.

Baking soda and vinegar can be used to clean baked-on food from pots and pans. A plastic putty blade can be used to remove scum from bathroom surfaces. Mold can be removed from silicone sealants on bathtubs and washbasins by applying bleach to the surface, letting it sit for an hour or more, and then rinsing thoroughly.

Brush the joints between tiles with a toothbrush and liquid soap. Sugar soap is also an effective paint remover and can also remove odors. Pour an industrial-strength, high-quality, rust-removing solution inside the toilet bowl, let it sit for 30 minutes, and flush. Alternatively, Coke can be used. Make sure you thoroughly clean your shower and sink drains with baking soda or commercial drain cleaner. Chrome taps can be polished by rubbing them with toothpaste and water, followed by rinsing. If the drain is rusted, you can pour a rust-removing agent (or ketchup) on it and wipe it clean after 30 minutes.

Clean and sanitize your washing machine by selecting the longest cycle, setting it for the biggest load (but do not fill it) at the hottest temperature with a quarter cup of bleach added, and repeat with a quarter cup of white vinegar.

Shut the windows and doors and run an air purifier for a couple of hours to eliminate musty odors and tobacco smells. The mildew spores will be killed, and the scent will be permanently eliminated.

Empty the garbage bins regularly. Guests should not smell rotten food after opening the trash can to dispose of their trash.

Cover your pillows and mattresses and wash the covers regularly to keep them protected. Towels should be white so that stains can be easily removed. Adding a few drops of white vinegar to your wash will keep colors bright, ensure whites are white, and produce fluffy towels.

Putting a little dish of baking soda in the refrigerator cabinet and changing it frequently can help control refrigerator odors. You can use a lint roller or sticky tape to remove stubborn dirt, dust, and pet hair from clothing and furniture. Bacteria thrive in hair dryers and remote controls. Thoroughly clean them after each guest.

Clean behind the bedside tables every time you have a guest. If the outlets are hidden under tables, customers can take them out and plug in their appliances. Dust, dirt, and leftover food left behind by past occupants will not disappear on their own. Light bulbs should be cleaned, in particular, the bulbs in nightstand lamps. Magnetism in these devices can attract dust, and dust can accumulate and cause fires.

Your guests' first impression of your newly acquired apartment will be shaped by the outside of your property. Do everything in your power to impress them right away.

FURNISHING AND DECORATING YOUR SPACE

Budgeting goes beyond rent, security deposit, and insurance. It also involves creating a memorable space for your guests. Now is the perfect time to make your home more comfortable, attractive, and hospitable. Consider these questions:

- What feelings would I like my guests to experience during their stay?
- What can I do to make their visit more comfortable and enjoyable?

Once you determine what you want, you can create a stunning home. In terms of furniture, you have several options.

Rent a Furnished Space

Setting up a business can be challenging and time-consuming. The same is true for setting up a rental property. A furnished space is the best way to get a return on investment in nine days. Furnished homes usually have a higher rental rate.

However, renting a fully furnished home will save you time and money. You will spend less money upfront and can use the extra cash on amenities to upgrade your home.

Rent Furniture on a Short-Term Basis

When it comes to designing your rental home, renting furniture for a short period of time is an excellent option and provides flexibility. You can have your property furnished for as little as one month, with the option to renew every month. Once you start earning some money, you can buy your own furniture.

Buy Furniture

Subletting an Airbnb apartment without furniture will require you to purchase items such as tables, chairs, and bedding to furnish the apartment. The cost may vary from $5,000 to $10,000, depending on the size of the property.

Purchasing used household items is an inexpensive way to do this. Keep in mind that the smaller your upfront costs for an item, the more likely you will need to replace it.

Amenities

Would you like to know what amenities get your guests' attention, make them feel special, and generate a lot of interest? I've read through guest comments, responses, and reviews, and I've talked to hundreds of my own guests to get a sense of what makes them feel at home. I've compiled this list of amenities based on my experience to help you impress your guests and get awesome reviews.

▷ WiFi

Most Airbnbs consider internet access to be the most important amenity. Once a guest arrives, it's very important they can access WiFi. Internet speed is crucial unless you are marketing your space as a "retreat" from the daily grind.

▷ Smart TV with Subscriptions

A smart TV with Internet connectivity that can stream content is an excellent addition. Providing your guests with streaming services like Netflix is an added bonus.

▷ In-Home Speakers

Having an in-home speaker that guests can conveniently connect to and enjoy is another unique amenity they appreciate. Most people enjoy listening to music when they're unwinding at home. It may not be a standard item, so guests won't expect to see it. However, it makes a positive impact if they have the option.

▷ Professional Cleaning Service

Managing your short-term rental property during and after each guest stay, building your Airbnb business, and responding to guest inquiries are all time-consuming tasks. By hiring a professional cleaning company, you can rest assured that professionals handle your business' cleaning.

▷ Utilities

In addition to cleaning up after each guest and repairing any damage, you must also consider the cost of utilities. Utility costs are perhaps the highest variable cost. Make sure they are properly set up and paid on time.

Using a smart thermostat for your Airbnb, you can save up to 20% on your heating and cooling bills (Kaylee, 2019). This is also a great way to make sure your guests are comfortable as soon as they walk through the door. Several smart thermostats are available on the market and are relatively easy to install. Below are some easy ways to save money on your electricity bill if you have a smart thermostat:

- When your guest leaves, turn off the heat or air conditioning using your smartphone.
- Warm-up or cool your home a couple of hours before your guests arrive, so they don't have to adjust the temperature themselves.
- Set the minimum and maximum temperatures guests can select.
- If you have an automatic sensor, you can lower the thermostat when a window or door is left open for too long.

▷ Toiletries

On Airbnb, the little things sometimes make the difference between a decent guest experience and a truly exceptional one. Let's talk about toiletries. What kind of toilet paper do you have? Does it feel soft? Is there shampoo?

In the amenities section of your Airbnb listing, you will find a box labeled "Essentials." The essentials are soap, shampoo, and conditioner. You can't check that you have the "essentials" if you don't provide these items. These items are relatively inexpensive and will make your guests' experience more pleasant. Although it may not be the shampoo they use, people appreciate the effort.

▷ Kitchenware

Is it possible to provide guests with fresh coffee? Sugar and tea? With coffee pods, guests can enjoy coffee without having to grind it themselves. Using coffee pods has many benefits, but don't overlook their quality. Providing your guests with additional spatulas, wooden spoons, can openers, wine openers, and other kitchen items can make their stay more comfortable. I provide everything guests need to prepare meals and clean up afterward - Airbnb offers guests the convenience of not having to go out to eat for every meal.

Remember the golden rule: Make your guests feel as comfortable as you would like to feel at home. Make sure to provide toiletries and supplies you would have at home. Generally, guests won't expect you to go above and beyond what you can reasonably offer. Still, you may consider providing a little something extra to guests who have shown a particular interest in your property.

Airbnb is built on reviews, and reviews are trusted by both parties. Showing more supplies, amenities, and toiletries than you actually offer is not a good idea. Your listing is rated based on the information you provide, so being honest about your listing while surprising your guests will really make your listing stand out! If you use these little-known strategies to provide your Airbnb guests with an unforgettable stay, you will be well on your way to generating more income as your unit gains popularity.

ROOM-BY-ROOM PLAYBOOK

The most sought-after Airbnb's offer all the comforts of home but better. As a host, you should strive to provide your guests with a memorable experience that will keep them coming back. Let's talk about how to revamp the most important spaces in your rental that will really impress your guests.

How to Create a Great Bedroom in an Airbnb:

The bedroom in your rental requires a different design concept than that of a hotel or your own home. Airbnb bedroom furniture and decor must be sturdy enough to withstand repeated use and easy to replace if damaged.

▷ The Best Mattress

Poor mattress quality is one of the biggest reasons for poor reviews. No matter where they stay, whether a hotel or an Airbnb, your guests will notice the quality of the mattress.

▷ **The Bed frame**

Mattresses are only as good as their frames. They complement each other. An Airbnb bedroom is incomplete without a comfortable mattress and bed frame.

▷ **High-Quality Bed Sheets**

The bedding should be arranged in the following order: top sheet, flat sheet, then top layer. High-quality bedding is guaranteed to be admired and praised. In addition to being noticeable, high-quality beddings are long-lasting and easier to take care of.

▷ **Each Guest is Provided With two Pillows**

Airbnb requires you to provide one pillow per guest. You should provide one pillow and one decorative pillow per guest. Everyone has different preferences when it comes to pillows. The option of a memory foam pillow or a goose feather pillow will make every guest happy.

▷ **Wardrobe**

Rooms are often not spacious enough to unpack. Having the ability to unpack immediately helps guests feel at home. Consider placing a slim dresser or wardrobe in the Airbnb bedroom if the closet is too small. Don't forget clothes hangers.

▷ Carbon Monoxide Detector Is a Must

Most countries require you to install a smoke detector and carbon monoxide detector. They are often combined, making setup and maintenance easier.

▷ A Safe

If you have stayed in a luxurious hotel, you know how valuable a safe is. Generally, guests will keep their passports, money, and other valuables in a safe. They should feel confident that their personal property and valuable documents are secure.

▷ Theme

Your bedroom theme should be reflected in the overall design of your rental property. If your house has a boho aesthetic, your bedrooms should be decorated accordingly, with textures, patterns, and colors. While each room should have its own personality, it should also be integrated into the overall design. Make sure each bedroom appears unique so that it does not look like all bedrooms are identical.

The most popular themes are boho, glam, Victorian-era, modern minimalist, beachy, nautical, and farmhouse/rustic. You should choose a theme that isn't too peculiar or so specific that visitors will be discouraged from staying (Kamp, 2022).

▷ The Basics

No matter how you decorate a bedroom, it won't matter if it lacks basic necessities. These are must-haves:

- Mirror, full-length
- Hangers for clothing
- Rack for luggage
- Curtains for privacy
- Waste bin

▷ No Clutter

Clutter is the last thing you need in your bedroom. The room might appear cluttered and unattractive if there are too many elements. In addition, clutter makes cleaning and tidying up after guests more difficult. You will have less work to do if you keep things simple and clean.

How to Create an Awesome Living Space in an Airbnb:

No matter how large or small your Airbnb property is, the living room is likely to be the feature that makes it all come together. It's also likely that your guests will spend the most time in this room (besides the bedroom), which means it'll be the first room they think of when they remember their Airbnb stay.

▷ Couch

Much like when choosing a seating arrangement for your home, you must do your research thoroughly. If you select a couch that is not durable, you may end up paying too much or having to replace it soon. You should consider a slipcover for the sofa. Make your dirty or torn couch look brand new with a high stretch slipcover! You won't even have to explain the slipcover to renters; most likely, they won't even realize it. Furthermore, slipcovers can be used to change the style of your living room and make cleaning much easier!

▷ Coffee Table

There should be a convenient place for guests to set down their cup of water or glass of wine. Even if your living room is small, you might consider placing a small table behind the seating area, which can accommodate a few coasters, a few magazines, and remote control (The Airbnb Host's Living Room Essentials Checklist, 2018).

▷ Lighting

Lighting plays a vital role in the guest experience. It is also aesthetically pleasing. Light fixtures come in simple and neutral colors and elaborate and colorful ones. When enticing your Airbnb guests, choosing the right lighting is crucial.

▷ Local Experience

Sometimes guests are unsure what they want to see, when to visit, how to get there, etc. Providing your guests with brochures, maps, city suggestions, and relevant information is a great idea to help them navigate and enjoy their visit.

▷ Games

Isn't it great when a board game brings people together? Young travelers may prefer to spend time outdoors, but parents with young children may find these games to be a delightful way to keep them entertained indoors.

How to Set Up the Perfect Kitchen in an Airbnb:

Airbnbs are popular with travelers because they offer the convenience of having their own kitchen (Lavie, 2020). To save money, they can store leftovers from dining out in the fridge or make a meal at home. Restaurant dining can be challenging for people who are allergic to certain foods or have dietary restrictions. Regardless of the situation, it's crucial that you know what to have on hand to prepare your kitchen for guests.

▷ A Basic set of Utensils

You will need the following tools: a wooden spoon, a plastic spatula, a whisk, a big soup spoon, and tongs. All of which should be heat-resistant. Additionally, you'll need several openers: a wine opener, a can opener, and a bottle opener.

▷ Dishes and Cups

You will need the following: bowls, plates, cups, and mugs. A variety of plate sizes is helpful. When determining the number of each dish you need to have on hand, consider the following: How many guests will be staying at your rental? At the very least, everyone should be able to attend dinner together.

▷ Mixing Bowls

If you've ever made eggs in a coffee cup or fruit salad in a cake pan, you'll understand why it's so convenient to have a mixing bowl or two when you're staying at an Airbnb. Having a set of bowls grouped together is great.

▷ Morning Brew

When guests first wake up in your Airbnb, they usually head straight to the kitchen for their morning coffee. You should have an electric kettle, Keurig, or regular coffee maker. If you are the kind of host who goes above and beyond by providing tea and coffee to your guests, you might want to provide sugar and creamer. Guests who enjoy a quick caffeine boost in the morning will appreciate your consideration.

▷ Chef's Knives and Large Cutting Board

The most frequently forgotten necessity in Airbnb kitchens are knives. Make your guests feel at home by providing them with knives and a large cutting board. You can purchase a universal knife block to store them in. Don't let them slosh around in the cupboard and lose their luster. Sharpen your knives regularly.

▷ Pots

A small and a large pot are ideal. The pot should be small enough to work as a saucepan and large enough to handle a few cups of rice or a batch of stew. Each pot should have a matching lid.

▷ Pans

You should have two pans: a circular pan and a sheet pan, so your guests can prepare whatever dessert or savory dish they want.

How to Set Up a Gorgeous Bathroom in an Airbnb

It may seem that bathrooms are a simple area to design, but it has a lot of potential to wow your guests and make your Airbnb stand out from the crowd. A well-equipped bathroom makes guests feel more comfortable. Even if no one notices your decorations or looks in the kitchen, your guests will appreciate the time and effort you put into organizing the bathroom.

▷ Toilet Paper

It is unlikely that your guests will notice what brand of toilet paper you use, but they will notice when it runs out. Make sure your guests have extra toilet paper if they plan to stay for a week or more.

The standard practice is to provide guests one roll of toilet paper every two nights (Universe, 2018). You can place additional tissue rolls on top of the toilet or install a holder to hold extra rolls. You can also buy tissue wholesale or on sale to provide your guests with high-quality toilet paper at an affordable price.

▷ A Beautiful set of Towels

Towels should be provided to every guest. If your property has a swimming pool, sauna, or gym, make sure you have extra towels for guests when they feel like swimming or exercising.

Also, let guests know where to place their used towels so that housekeeping can easily access them. It will prevent dirty towels from being tucked away in closets and forgotten.

▷ Toiletries

A bathroom should have toiletries such as shampoo, soap, and body wash. You should avoid using fragrance-based or scented soaps. You might have guests who are allergic to chemicals.

▷ Hooks

Hooks are a must-have for your Airbnb bathroom. Guests should be able to hang wet towels and clothes on hooks behind the door. Additionally, you can place hooks near the shower so guests can quickly grab their towels after showering.

▷ Bath Mats

You should install bath mats in spots that get wet to prevent slipping. Bath mats can prevent slips and keep your floors dry at the same time.

▷ Wastebasket

There should always be a wastebasket in the bathroom so people can easily dispose of waste. Remember to remind your guests to dispose of trash according to your house rules.

Be Sensible

Imagine everything you would want to have if you were on vacation, and make it available for your guests. Also, consider who will be staying at your facility and what amenities they might need. If you expect guests with children, and depending on where your property is located, you may want to provide a stowaway crib and durable dishes. If your vacation rental is located in a party-loving city such as Miami, you might want to have extra jiggers.

PHYSICAL HANDBOOK

Your guests' first impression of your Airbnb can make the difference between a memorable stay and a forgettable one. Make your guests feel welcome with a personalized welcome guide.

Welcome Page

The first thing they'll see is the welcome page! When I host guests, I like to include these things to make them feel comfortable and welcome. Setting the tone and introducing your guests to your home is important.

My welcome page includes my address, contact information, and the number of people my Airbnb accommodates.

Other details you should include are:

- Detailed parking information
- Access codes
- Wi-Fi information
- Emergency contact information

House Rules

In addition to your listing, your Airbnb's house rules are equally important. In your handbook, you should provide guidelines and details about your home and rules to guests. I have developed my house rules over the years as a result of my different interactions with guests.

Some hosts have very detailed rules. They may have a long list to follow, from "clean the shower after your shower" to "no hot water after 5pm." A long list of rules can be overwhelming, and discussing some points in person is best.

Guests may want to know:

- Can I bring a friend?
- Can they stay overnight?
- Can I smoke on the property?
- Can I have an event?
- Can I bring my pet?

Questions to Get You Thinking

Here are some questions to help you think about what you want to include in your Airbnb rules:

- Will you allow smoking inside your property?
- Are pets allowed?
- Will guests have to take off their shoes?
- Can guests use the washing/dryer? If so, do you charge them?
- Are there quiet hours?
- Can guests' friends stay over?
- Is it okay to eat in the bedroom?

Take your landlord's rules into consideration. Also, consider the type of travelers you may have when writing your house rules.

A Template for Airbnb House Rules

Use this foolproof house rules template to create your own.

- No loud music
- No smoking
- No pets
- No parties
- If you break it, fix it

- Not suitable for children and infants [if applicable]
- No eating or drinking in bedrooms
- Please turn off the air conditioning when not using
- You are required to check-in and out at the scheduled times
- Please handle your keys with care. If your keys are lost, you will be charged.
- Please take out the trash before leaving
- No illegal substances are allowed

Rules are a must for you, the landlord, and guests. By having them, you set expectations for your guests. It is crucial to provide your guests with rules to ensure your property's safety and peace of mind.

Transportation Options in the Area

Next, you should have a section explaining how guests can get around. You might tell your guests whether Uber is available. You can also tell them if there are any unique transportation options available. You should provide any information your visitors might want to know about transportation options.

Things to Do

Share your favorite local dining spots! You can recommend your favorite restaurants, nightclubs, and coffee shops they might enjoy. You can also share things you enjoy doing around the area.

Provide them with the cost of each activity. Include an activity if you think it's worth their time! Another thing you could do is include the distance between each location on foot or by car. Guests can then know how long it will take them to travel.

Electronic Devices and Appliances

Finally, guests will want to know how to use any electronic devices in your Airbnb. You might include information about TV or Netflix passwords. When it comes to electronics, it is a good rule of thumb to explain it the same way you would to your grandmother. You might find it easy to use, but someone visiting your home for the first time might find it confusing. Ensure you provide detailed troubleshooting instructions and any other information they need to use the electronic devices in your home.

No matter where your business is located or who your guests are, it is crucial that you create a handbook that is available on-site and on your Airbnb listing.

6

CREATING YOUR LISTING AND OPTIMIZING IT FOR SUCCESS

I n order to host guests on Airbnb, you must first list your property on the website. Airbnb listings allow potential guests to learn more about your home and make reservations. A listing includes photos and property details. It's easy to list your property! To create your listing, give yourself a day and a few more to polish it.

CREATING YOUR AIRBNB LISTING

You will need to enter the address of your property and some basic information when you sign up for Airbnb.

Click "list your property." Create an Airbnb account if you don't already have one. If Airbnb detects your location by your IP address, you will see the average weekly income from nearby properties. That's a great incentive to continue listing your property! If necessary, you can change the "default" city. You can see how the weekly income changes depending on the accommodation type: a) private room, b) whole house, or c) shared room.

LET'S START WITH THE BASICS

Here is a list of questions you should be prepared to answer.

- Is this listing for a private residence, a hotel, or something else?

Your choices for the remaining questions will be based on your answer.

- What kind of property is this?
- What will the guests have access to (the entire property, shared room, shared room)?
- Is this property primarily used as a vacation home?
- How many guests can stay on the property?
- How many beds are there?
- What size of beds are available (queen, double, single)?

- How many bathrooms are there?
- What is the address?
- Verify on a map
- What do the different room types mean?

Airbnb offers three types of accommodations:

Shared accommodation: Guests share a room with their hosts or roommates and do not have a separate bedroom.

Private room: Visitors have access to some communal spaces (i.e., dining room, living room, toilet); however, there is a separate sleeping area.

Entire Home: Renters get the whole property and do not have to share it with anyone.

You are responsible for providing accurate information about your property and selecting the correct accommodation type.

SPECIFY THE LOCATION

You'll enter the property address and verify the location. I won't insult your intelligence by explaining how to type an address.

AMENITIES

Now it's time to highlight the property's amenities.

Safety amenities are essential to guests, and in most places, they are a legal requirement, so you should be prepared to have the following:

- Emergency First Aid Kit
- Smoke detector
- CO detector
- Fire extinguisher
- A lockable bedroom door

Fire extinguishers and smoke detectors improve your home's safety and make your listing stand out.

NUMBER OF GUESTS

It is your responsibility to ensure your guests' comfort. So, be aware of the number of guests you can accommodate. Consider how many beds or other sleeping spaces you have.

THE SPACES THAT GUESTS CAN USE

Make a list of all the facilities, and rooms guests will have access to while staying at your property.

PROPERTY DESCRIPTION AND TITLE

A detailed description of your property is essential for a successful Airbnb listing. Create a memorable short-term rental property by being creative and showing the guests what they can expect from your temporary accommodation.

In the title: The listing name should be no more than 50 characters. Get your listing noticed!

Summary: Describe the interior, lighting, nearby attractions, etc.

The space: Describe what makes your home unique.

Guest interaction: Be sure to let guests know you are available to help.

Other things to note: Provide guests with any additional information pertinent to their stay.

The neighborhood: Besides pictures, provide guests with information about the area.

My place is great for: Families (with children), Large groups, and Pets.

PICTURE PERFECT AIRBNB PHOTOS

When listing your space, photographs are crucial. Outstanding photos give potential guests a better sense of your property and give you an edge over competitors (boring images can make your listing appear unattractive). You should take good pictures of your listing since most potential guests will book based on pictures. The quality of your photos will determine whether you have frequent bookings or not.

It's not enough to take a few good photos with your phone. There is a big difference between poor and exceptional photography. It can be pretty noticeable. Ineffective photos hurt your listing and keep it from reaching its full potential.

When you take pictures of your home, make sure it is staged correctly. If your space doesn't look great, your photos won't look great either.

A well-staged property is crucial to a positive guest experience. When guests view your advertisement, they should be able to imagine themselves there. Your pictures should entice them to view your listing. Staging lets your guests experience your space from the comforts of their own home.

Make it feel like home by paying attention to every detail. Airbnb guests prefer accommodations that align with the company's philosophy of living like a local. This is the opposite of what hotels offer. Imagine Airbnb as a home away from home. When it comes to staging your space as a home, keeping your local identity is important.

KEEP YOUR SPACE IMMACULATE

As mentioned previously, maintaining a clean and well-maintained space is essential. Hire a cleaning service before taking pictures. Make sure the cleaners go the extra mile to make your space look good.

Arrange everything so that everything is in its place. Make the space look like a magazine spread. When staging, consider these factors:

- Check that your rugs and chairs are aligned and that everything is placed correctly.
- Hide any cables.
- Ensure the pillows on the couch and bed are fluffy and arranged properly.
- You can also iron the sheets to prevent wrinkles.
- Remove any tags from your sheets or pillowcases.

- Close the shower curtain and the toilet lid.
- If your shower is appealing, you might want to take a moment to take pictures. Try to keep the bathroom closed, so it looks more spacious and neat.

With a few little touches like these, your photos will look amazing. It will make your guests choose your space over your competitors.

LEVEL-UP YOUR STAGING

Stage your space to make it feel like a home. Consider adding flowers or plants. A newspaper and a bowl of fruit and coffee on the table will help your guests imagine themselves in your kitchen, enjoying breakfast and catching up on the news. Your space will really stand out when you add subtler and more detailed touches.

HIGHLIGHT THE SELLING POINTS AND BE HONEST ABOUT THE DOWNSIDES

There's always a temptation to exaggerate the quality of your rental, but it's never a good idea. A bad Airbnb experience begins with not being honest about your listing. In most cases, an inaccurate description that paints an unreliable impression of your property will only lead to negative reviews. Tell your guests what they can expect from your Airbnb in your listing.

Details about the property should be provided, such as the number of rooms and the features of each room, including bed sizes, closet space, etc. Inform guests about your property's amenities, accommodations, and advantages.

Establish some guidelines or rules, such as whether guests can bring pets or additional guests, whether smoking is allowed, and whether certain areas of the house are off-limits. Keep things simple, and similarly, in terms of photography, being truthful is more important than impressing your clients with false images.

DESCRIBE YOUR HOUSE RULES

We discussed house rules previously. In addition to an appealing description, eye-catching pictures, and a compelling introduction to your Airbnb listing, Airbnb house rules are equally critical. It is OK to give guests rules about what they can do in your home.

Additionally, your rules for visitors are a marketing tool. They let travelers know whether your accommodation is suitable for them. And if they are a good match for you.

PRICING AND AVAILABILITY

If you are renting out your own property rather than a separate space, then you should decide how frequently you would like to rent it out, how much notice you will need before your guests' arrival, and the minimum and maximum stay period.

Airbnb sets a minimum stay requirement that specifies how many nights your guests can stay.

Booking one-night stays on your Airbnb listing may result in more bookings, but it may also bring in less reliable guests. One-night stays have a tendency to become party houses.

Most hosts list their listings for three nights (iGMS, 2020). This keeps occupancy rates high and attracts responsible travelers.

CANCELLATION POLICY

Next, you'll select from one of the six different cancellation policies on Airbnb.

Flexible: Cancellations are permitted up to 14 days before the check-in date (the time is shown in the confirmation email). If you book less than 14 days before check-in, cancellations are free for 48 hours following booking and 24 hours before check-in. If a cancellation is requested within 24 hours of arrival, guests will receive a refund of the room and cleaning fees, excluding service charges. Having a reasonable cancellation policy will help you get your first bookings when you begin your hosting venture. Travelers will benefit most from this refund policy since it offers the most flexibility.

Moderate: Cancellation is free up to 14 days before check-in. Cancellations are free up to 48 hours before booking, five days prior to check-in, if booked less than 14 days in advance. Guests can cancel up to five days prior to arrival and receive a refund of the accommodation and cleaning fee, but not the service fee.

Strict: Free cancellation for 48 hours, provided the cancellation is made at least 14 days before check-in. Guests can cancel up to seven days in advance and receive a 50% cancellation fee of the room charge and the cleaning fee, excluding the service fee.

Long Term: When reservations exceed 28 nights. Airbnb offers a full refund minus the first 30 days and the service fee if guests cancel before check-in.

Super strict 30 days: Cancellations must be made 30 days in advance, and guests will receive a 50% refund on the accommodation and cleaning fee, excluding the service fee. However, this policy is only available to some hosts in exceptional circumstances.

Super strict 60 days: Cancellations must be made at least 60 days prior to check-in, and guests will receive a 50% reimbursement of the accommodation and cleaning fee, excluding service charges. Only certain hosts are eligible for this policy.

ADDITIONAL FEES

Airbnb hosts can add additional fees. There are cleaning fees, security deposits, and extra guest fees.

Cleaning Fees

It is a common misconception that charging too high cleaning fees or a fair market rate discourages customers from booking. This is not true. It results in a similar amount of bookings and revenue regardless of the fact that your cleaning rates are much lower than or comparable to your competitors. However, when you price too high over the average price for cleaning services, you are more likely to lose bookings.

Security Deposit

Your security deposit should be adequate to protect yourself against loss or damage to your property. You won't need to touch your liability insurance or Airbnb's insurance. The security deposit for an average rental property should not be less than $150 or $200.

Additional Guest fee

It is possible to set up an additional guest fee. You only need to specify what you want to charge for other guests and how many guests are allowed. This fee can be included in your pricing, but I would only suggest doing so if you have incurred extra costs because of the additional guest. You don't want your guests to feel taken advantage of.

INSTANT BOOK

Whenever possible, Instant Book should be enabled. You should only disable Instant Book if maximizing bookings is not your priority. If Airbnb is just a personal interest for you, and you value the freedom, it gives you more than the financial benefit it provides, turn it off. Disable Instant Book and take control back.

PERFECTING YOUR AIRBNB PROFILE

Describe your role as a host, and explain why guests should trust you. In addition to uploading a professional picture of yourself, you can provide a phone number where Airbnb can reach you, and your guests can also see this information.

You must also verify your listing with Airbnb to prevent fake listings. There are several ways to verify your listing. Completing all verification steps will make your listing more credible and trustworthy (iGMS, 2020). Completing your profile and submitting the appropriate verifications will make travelers less nervous about booking your property.

PROVEN TIPS TO BOOST YOUR AIRBNB SEO

Now that your listing is set up let's focus on optimizing it. Airbnb SEO is a way to increase the visibility of your listing on Airbnb's search engine results pages. Ranking higher on Airbnb is achieved by meeting the search engine's ranking standards. Airbnb has publicly disclosed several ranking guidelines, although many remain secret. Understanding Airbnb's ranking system (and the factors that affect it) will help you control your ranking on Airbnb's search results page.

1. Respond to Your Guests Promptly

Your response rate is measured by responding promptly to booking requests and answering your guests' questions via Airbnb's message system. This does not require any special skills. Always respond to messages. A simple "thank you" counts. It may happen that you are not interested in their question or are not interested in accepting the booking. Instead of ignoring their request, you should explain why you cannot accept their reservation.

2. Maintain an up-to-date Calendar

Regularly update your calendar. When you know you will have difficulty hosting on a particular date, block out the date on your calendar. Plan ahead and mark any potential conflicting dates as soon as possible, rather than waiting until you are pressed for time. You should only have your calendar open when you want people to make a booking.

3. Increase the Number of 5-star reviews

Everything depends on your rating. Maintaining a high rating requires providing the best possible service consistently (I'll discuss this more in-depth later).

4. Use Instant Book

According to Airbnb, if you activate Instant Booking, you can increase bookings by 20%. In addition, it's a good way to get last-minute reservations, which make up about 40% of bookings (Smartbnb, 2021).

5. Avoid Refusals and Cancellations

AirBnB's SEO boost comes from cancellations, which are calculated by dividing the number of canceled bookings by the number of total reservations. Despite having a high booking rate, a few mistakes can cause you to lose business.

6. Update Your Airbnb Profile Regularly

You need a complete listing and host profile to optimize your Airbnb listing. Bookings are more likely to occur when listings have more information since guests want to feel secure and book with hosts they can trust. Verify your listing and make sure to fill in every detail correctly.

7. Utilize Social Media to Promote Your Account

You should also promote your Airbnb listing on social media after you have created it. Share it on your social networks and tell your family and friends about it. Maintaining a social media presence is essential to Airbnb SEO. Airbnb will immediately appreciate your move, boosting your ranking (GMS, 2016). External links are extremely beneficial to your search engine ranking. So, promote your business on other platforms in addition to Airbnb.

8. Create a Comprehensive Guidebook

Airbnb guides are a great way to increase your Airbnb search engine rankings, attract guests, and make their stay more enjoyable. Airbnb is popular not just because of the accommodations but also because of the hosts' knowledge of local attractions. The majority of your guests are unlikely to be locals. They aren't familiar with the local "must-see" attractions you might know! This allows you to provide a higher level of customer service by providing them with a local guide's knowledge.

9. Invest in Professional Photos

Hiring a skilled photographer is one of the most important steps in creating an Airbnb listing. Your photos should not be skimped on; instead, hire a qualified photographer for all your listings. Always. It is important to know that taking your own pictures or hiring a professional photographer will play a massive role in attracting reservations

10. Offer Competitive Prices

The first few months are the most challenging. When you plan to match your competitors' amenities and overall offerings, you will have the advantage when you charge less than they do. As you begin your journey, you should aim to build momentum rather than maximize earnings from any booking.

7

MAXIMIZING PROFITS AND KEEPING YOUR SPACE FULLY BOOKED

Airbnb pricing is not as simple as it seems. There is more to it than you might think. New hosts often choose their pricing haphazardly and adopt a passive pricing strategy, which can negatively impact their rankings in search engines. Understanding how Airbnb prices are affected by different factors is key to setting the right price. When developing your pricing plan, if one of these factors is overlooked, it can lead to fewer bookings and lower profits. It will be a process of fine tuning, which can be completed within two days of posting your listing.

WHAT IS THE TOTAL NUMBER OF ROOMS, AND HOW MANY GUESTS CAN YOU ACCOMMODATE?

Because each guest has different needs and desires, it's sometimes difficult to determine the best price. How many people can you accommodate in your home, and how does your home look? Renting an entire home, apartment, or condo is typically more expensive than renting a shared space. The price of your property should be similar to the ones in your area. You can filter Airbnb to see how much rent in similar properties usually goes for.

Airbnb has four types of arrangements, each indicating the kind of accommodation offered. Generally, entire homes cost more, with the average Airbnb rate in 2021 being $149/night. On average, shared Airbnb rooms cost $44 per night (All The Rooms Analytics, n.d.).

WHAT IS THE LOCATION OF YOUR PROPERTY?

How would you describe the neighborhood where your property is? Would you be interested in visiting the area if you didn't live there? What are the nearby attractions? Airbnb properties should be near local attractions and services that will enhance a guest's stay. What are some of the most popular bars, cafes, and coffee shops to check out during a weekend getaway? Can the telecommuting, extended-stay guest find a nearby grocery store or exercise facility? Is there a playground or ice cream parlor nearby for families on vacation? Are there hiking trails or outdoor activities nearby? Your price should reflect all of the benefits and drawbacks of your property. Airbnbs should appeal to a specific niche, and if your property has a nearby amenity that guests would find appealing, that's a big plus.

WHAT AMENITIES DO YOU OFFER?

Guests may not be aware of the amenities you include in your prices. For example, the safety and beauty of your neighborhood may not be known to a stranger unfamiliar with your area, so make sure you emphasize these factors. You can also increase your rates by including extra touches, such as breakfast or a welcome basket with treats, but you must be very clear about them when you list your home.

WHO ARE YOUR TARGET GUESTS?

Can guests relax in the hot tub outside while enjoying a spectacular lake view? Is there a five-star outdoor kitchen where they can grill steaks? What about a fireplace made of real wood and a game room in the basement? These kinds of unique amenities appeal to prospective travelers.

You can influence the price of your Airbnb property by choosing the right audience. Imagine that your Airbnb property features luxurious amenities to entice guests with large bank accounts. If you provide a luxury experience, you should charge the maximum amount. If you cater to budget-conscious customers like students, your nightly rates should reflect what they expect to pay. Decide which groups of guests you can accommodate. Traveling nurses, parents with children, honeymooners, and business owners are all possible applicants. Every traveler has different expectations, so their experiences will differ. Airbnb accommodations should be tailored to the travelers' needs. You can estimate the nightly rate based on the type of customer you are targeting.

WHAT ARE YOUR COMPETITORS' PRICES?

Airbnb's standard search feature can help you find comparable properties nearby. Search for properties based on the number of bedrooms and guests you intend to have.

If a property is already reserved, it will not appear in your search results. Try searching for dates three to six months in the future. For the best results, search for a stay of at least three days and no longer than a week.

First bookings can seem scary. However, it's easy to get started. Your first goal should be to increase your occupancy rate and get positive feedback from your guests. You want to get as many bookings and positive reviews from guests as quickly as possible. Initially, there are no bookings or feedback about your property. In general, prospective guests prefer to book accommodations that have reviews.

Use the following pricing strategy to increase your listing's momentum during your expansion phase. Set your price 20% below what competitors in your area are charging. This undervalues your listing compared to your competitors. Give it a week and see if your space is mostly booked for the next two weeks.

If your listing is mainly booked in the next two weeks, keep marketing it at the low price until it is mostly booked one month in advance - aim for 80% occupancy or more. If you are not booked, lower your price by 10% each week until you are. Once you're fully booked four weeks or more in advance, raise your rates 10% a week until you're fully booked for the following four weeks or until you reach the standard rate in your area.

Your listing's profile name and details should indicate that it is new. It will help guests understand why you don't have any reviews and why your listing is so cheap compared to your competitors. Once you have a few listings and a few 5-star reviews, you can raise your prices. Keeping up with price changes can be difficult, but here are some steps you can take to make the process simpler.

SEASONALITY

When setting your prices, you may need to adjust them according to the season. Seasonality refers to the overall demand for Airbnb listings - vacancy rates and standard per-night rates may be higher or lower than their average rates during periods of increased or decreased demand.

It is not uncommon for a villa at a well-known beach resort to be rented almost every night, often at rates significantly higher than usual during the summer. Even at a significant discount, it is likely that this same villa will struggle to fill bookings during the low season when the sun isn't as bright.

KEEP YOUR BUSINESS GOALS AND OBJECTIVES IN MIND

Setting goals and targets as part of your business strategy will ensure that your Airbnb business will succeed in the short and long term. As you determine and develop your Airbnb pricing strategy, keep your goals in mind. If you have set a goal for the amount of profit you would like to generate monthly, you should price your property based on the income you need to achieve your goal, while taking into account your spending and occupancy expectations. If you set a goal of hosting a certain number of guests in your property every quarter, keep your rates competitive and make your property more appealing to travelers. Once you have established an average price, you should use a dynamic pricing tool to monitor and automatically adjust your rates.

DYNAMIC PRICING TOOLS

Although manual pricing helps determine average daily prices and accounts for seasonal changes and occurrences, it fails to take into account one of the most important components of optimal pricing: the current availability and pricing of your direct competitors.

In other words, your pricing should take into account your competitors' availability and pricing during any given night. For instance, if your competition has low rates on any given day, you may have difficulty booking your property. Similarly, if most of your competitors are booked, leaving fewer options for travelers, you will be able to charge more.

Since most listings are available two months in advance, there are roughly 300 nights to monitor occupancy and prices. To manually update your pricing would be impossible, never mind maintaining it. Therefore, I strongly recommend you use dynamic pricing tools to monitor market competition and price changes in real-time.

Airbnb's Smart Pricing is optimized to maximize bookings through the system, not to increase the revenue of specific listings like yours. Airbnb is a business that collects service fees from guests and hosts for each booking. However, it does not charge both parties the same. Airbnb charges hosts a flat fee of 3% of the gross booking amount and guests approximately 13% of the total (the nightly rate plus cleaning fee and any additional fees) (Symon He, 2020). Airbnb makes four times as much from guests as it does from hosts. Airbnb relies on fees as its primary source of revenue, so the company wants to keep its listing prices as low as possible to encourage travelers to book. That's precisely what Airbnb's Smart Pricing does. Your listings are always suggested at prices much lower than what they could actually command in your market.

Unlike Airbnb's Smart Pricing, dynamic pricing tools do not charge a service fee to guests. Instead, they receive a small commission from you. They will make more money if they can help you earn more. They have the same incentive as you do: to increase your earnings.

Pricelabs

PriceLabs is a pricing optimization tool for vacation rental properties. Hosts can set prices dynamically based on market conditions, demand, and seasonality.

Airbnb does not offer dynamic pricing, so each listing will have a fixed price that won't change until it is manually adjusted. It's a problem because you can't raise your rates when demand increases or lower them when demand decreases.

Using PriceLabs' pricing engine, you can set your prices automatically and understand your competitors' pricing strategies. If you dislike the prices set by Price-Lab, you can change them and choose your own rate. You will never be priced below your profit margins or priced out of your local market.

+ Advantages of PriceLabs

- With PriceLabs, you can generate graphs that provide visual suggestions and insights into pricing trends.
- You can set your own prices or follow PriceLabs' suggestions.
- The color-coded pricing calendar makes it easy to see when demand is high and low.
- Your price will be set according to your rules, so you won't have to worry about renting your Airbnb for less than you are willing to charge.
- Multiple listings can be managed from one centralized interface.
- PriceLabs integrates with more than 50 booking platforms, including Airbnb.

— Disadvantages of PriceLabs

- There are many features that can be confusing and difficult to use at first. You will have to learn the software before you can use it effectively.
- Since each listing is priced separately, the software can be pretty expensive.

PriceLabs is free, but you will only have access to the Portfolio analytics, not the Airbnb pricing analytics. PriceLabs charges $19.99 per listing for its dynamic pricing software. It is also free to try to see if it is right for you without committing. In addition to your subscription fee, you will need to pay an additional $9.99 per month for the market dashboard. Features of PriceLabs

Pricelabs has Three Main Features:

▷ **Dynamic Pricing**

Adjusts your rental rates automatically based on market conditions, demand, and profitability.

▷ **Portfolio Analytics**

Displays your vacation rental's KPIs and performance statistics.

▷ **Marketing Dashboard**

Analyze your market performance and evaluate properties before you invest.

If you are interested in dynamic pricing for your rentals, Beyond is another option.

Beyond

Beyond provides various services to help short-term landlords maximize their rental income. With Beyond's Dynamic Pricing algorithm, they can identify the three most important factors influencing demand at any given time: the local market, seasonality, and day of the week. An algorithm is then used to determine your property's rental price. With Dynamic Pricing, you will also have access to a wealth of historical information that will help you identify long-term trends in the market and use them to your advantage.

Beyond provides you with real-time market information that allows you to determine the best price to charge for your rental properties. The tool will enable you to see how other rental properties and hotels are pricing their properties in any given market and discover trends. The detailed filters allow you to customize and design your own charts based on your preferences, such as your preferred market and property size.

Among Their Other Tools are:

▷ **Relay**

A tool for managing listings and prices across multiple booking sites. Relay synchronizes pricing, availability, and bookings across various sites, making you more efficient.

▷ Signal

Beyond's property rental website builder and direct booking system. By using the system, you'll be able to keep more of the revenue collected from guests, eliminate expensive intermediaries, take advantage of repeat guests, and include package deals with reservations to maximize earnings. You can use this tool to customize your websites and make them more search engine friendly. Additionally, the service includes a WordPress website and booking management tools.

✛ Advantages of Beyond

- The ability to manage across different platforms
- A variety of analytical solutions and tactics
- Easily navigable and straightforward

━ Disadvantages of Beyond

- Due to the 1% to 1.49% fee charged for all reservations, fees can add up.
- It's not available in every market, and some regions are pretty broad.

At the end of each month, Beyond charges 1-1.49% of booking earnings. The fee is based on the number of bookings per month.

Without an automated system, it's impossible to analyze a large number of data points each day and calculate the best rate for each night. With dynamic pricing, low-demand nights are booked at lower rates, and high-demand nights are booked at higher rates, which results in higher occupancy and higher revenue for hosts.

WAYS TO BOOST YOUR REVENUE IN THE OFF-SEASON

Most rental properties, especially short-term accommodations, will experience vacancies at some point. I'm sure you're wondering what the best way to earn money in the off-season is? Are there any strategies to increase occupancy during the off-season? Here are a few of my favorite techniques for making money off-season.

Rent Your Property as an Event Space

You might want to consider renting your space through Peerspace or Splacer. Offering listings in towns and cities around the world, they are the industry's largest platforms for renting venues by the hour. Think

Airbnb, but for meetings, events, and gatherings. Worried your space won't be welcomed? Don't be! Whether you have a home, apartment, studio, or shed, you'll find guests.

During slow periods, you might consider listing your Airbnb property. The effectiveness of this method depends on where the property is located and how it looks. It might be worth a shot. Be sure to check with your landlord whether this is allowed.

You will create a listing with photos, a description, and pricing. When people rent your venue, they will be asked to leave feedback on their experience. Naturally, the cleaner, the more amenities, and the nicer the location, the more positive reviews and the greater the earning potential.

Put "Discount" in Your Airbnb Title

Many hosts change the title and details of their listings in the off-season to attract more guests. When travelers search for accommodations on Airbnb, you should use your listing title to grab their attention. When you list your property, use a seasonally-appropriate title to attract more guests.

Think of the title as representing your guests, not yourself. Since there will be so many Airbnb listings near you, you need to take every step possible to stand out.

Although your cover photo is important, your title is even more crucial, so optimize it to increase Airbnb views.

During slow seasons, you can add a phrase such as "Extra 15% Discount" to your title. When a guest has already filtered your listing to their preferred price range, and they see you are offering an additional 15% off, at the very least, it would be unthinkable not to check it out. Make sure you include the details of the discount in your listing.

Provide a 'Friends & Family' Discount

If you get guests during an off-season, let them know their family and friends can get a discount by mentioning the guest's name or using a code you provide. This can work really well in certain places.

You can even use an automated messaging tool to ensure that all your customers receive a message shortly after they check out.

Increase Percentage of Your Discounts

During the listing process, you can choose whether to offer discounts based on the length of stay, such as a week or a month. One simple trick is to boost the discounts to entice customers to book, especially those who are interested in staying longer. Most of your

Airbnb strategies will focus on increasing value for your guests during the off-season.

You don't have to compete on price all the time. You should strive to deliver the best quality and value for your guests. In the off-season, when things are tough, offering a competitive price is the best way to increase occupancy. Compare the percentage discounts your competitors offer in slow seasons and reduce yours even further.

Adjust the Minimum Stay

It can be annoying to host guests for only one night. In the off-season, however, people should have the option to book a single night. It's not as risky as you may think. When experiencing a tough season, take advantage of all the strategies you can use to increase occupancy. A few one-night stays could have a huge impact!

Eliminate Extra Person Fees

By eliminating the extra person charge, you remove another barrier to booking. Your first thought might be —"I'll lose a lot of moolah if I reduce rates and eliminate additional charges!" However, if no one books with you, you won't make any money either.

If you live in a seasonal location, you should remove as many barriers as possible. Having one more person in your rental won't add much to your workload. Yeah, you'll need an extra towel. Is it really worth an extra charge? As a host, you should make them feel like you want them to enjoy their stay, regardless of whether they have an additional guest.

Take Advantage of the Flexible Cancellation Policy

When times are slow, you want to loosen restrictions and rules as much as possible. You should give your guests as many options as possible when making a reservation. A strict cancellation policy can turn guests away. Most of your potential guests' concerns will be addressed if you have a flexible cancellation policy, use Instant Book, and remove extra charges.

If you want to succeed with Airbnb, you must know how to handle off-season bookings. It's essential to find creative ways to increase bookings and avoid losing revenue from an empty property.

MANAGING YOUR AIRBNB BUSINESS & SCALING TO SIX-FIGURE PROFITS

I n this chapter, I'll cover the process of maintaining your listings and how to scale your business. The basics of managing your listing are simple: If you provide a good experience for your guests, they will leave positive reviews, which will lead to more guests staying with you. You can be a great host by following these tips no matter how many listings you have.

AWESOME CUSTOMER SERVICE

Short-term rentals are popular among travelers because of their personalized experience and flexibility. Effective communication with them before entering your property can significantly enhance their experience.

Excellent customer service does not end when guests enter your property. Keeping guests informed throughout their stay is your responsibility. As soon as the guests arrive, ensure they are satisfied with their stay. Ask them to keep you informed if they have any concerns or issues. You can only resolve issues if you are aware of them. Here is a message I send halfway through their stay:

Dear Mary,

I am delighted to see you safely arrive at my home! I hope you enjoy your stay in Miami.
Please feel free to contact me with any comments, questions, or concerns. You can contact me by email (email address) or by phone (phone number). I will do my best to ensure that your stay is memorable.
Thank you for visiting, and enjoy your stay!
Kind regards,

Kay

When your guests depart, send the following message:

Dear Mary,

It was a pleasure having you stay in my apartment in Miami! Thank you so much for being such a lovely guest and being so respectful of my apartment.
Please feel free to contact me with any feedback or suggestions you may have since I am always looking for ways to improve my guests' experience.
I'd really appreciate it if you could leave a quick review on Airbnb. Reviews help potential guests make an informed decision about renting my apartment. Thank you very much!
I've also written a review for you. I wrote a positive review as you were a fantastic guest.
Wishing you all the best, and you're always welcome to stay at my apartment!
Kind regards,

Kay

Note that I specifically asked for feedback. When guests are satisfied, they are less likely to leave a review. A study found that one in ten satisfied guests will tell others about their experience, while unhappy guests will naturally tell 9-15 people about their disappointment (Thomas, 2018). Since I am seeking positive reviews, I ask my guests to leave reviews. Further, asking my guests for feedback provides me with valuable information about small faults that I might be able to fix.

CLEAN IT UP

In Chapter Five, I discussed the importance of keeping your place clean. It is not something you should overlook. You should always keep your place clean. Investing in a good cleaner is definitely worth the price. Aside from that, most people are less likely to damage an apartment that appears to be in good shape.

Today, many cleaning companies offer Airbnb cleanups as part of their regular cleaning services, and some cleaning companies specialize exclusively in Airbnb cleanups. Cleaning Airbnb properties is different from other cleaning services because it is usually done between 11am. and 3pm. Additionally, the steps must be followed precisely. Cleaners must be on time and complete their work before the arrival of new guests.

Cleaning an Airbnb listing also involves staging it to look its best to potential guests. Airbnb hosts have specific cleaning requirements, so hiring a traditional cleaning company can be difficult. By working with a company specializing in Airbnb turnovers, you can be assured that the cleaning staff knows their job and can handle your specific requirements.

KEEP IT SIMPLE

First, if you're renting out a space where you live, remove personal items that will not be useful to visitors. Don't leave your personal belongings lying around the property. You may want to store these items elsewhere:

- Clothing
- Personal hygiene products
- Electronics
- Footwear
- Fashion
- Personal documents
- Photographs

Consequently, there are certain items that your guests will find helpful. These are the items you should leave out:

- Reading material
- Films
- Video games

I have never had anything stolen from my properties, if you were curious. Keep your home clutter-free. A good Airbnb should feel like a home without being too personal. Don't display pictures of your family. The goal is to provide guests with a relaxing environment that allows them to kick back, unwind, and enjoy themselves.

KEEP GUESTS INFORMED

You should strive to be available at all times. Providing outstanding customer service requires being accessible and responsive. If people can't reach you, it won't matter how wonderful your property or listing is. In addition, as technology continues to advance, people have become increasingly impatient. Fast turnaround times and the ability to contact customer service immediately are becoming increasingly important.

Always respond to inquiries promptly. A good rule of thumb is to respond to each and every question within an hour of waking up. Set up an email alert so you will receive a notification as soon as an inquiry is received. I follow the one-hour rule every day, and my guests appreciate it. I'm sure your guests will be grateful as well.

Responding quickly is also extremely important since most users contact several hosts simultaneously.

An important part of providing a quick response is to still be thorough. When answering questions from your guests, it is important to be clear and concise. Unless you give them all the information they need to make an informed choice, you may lose out to your competitor. A helpful response to an inquiry would look like this:

Dear Mary,

I appreciate your interest in my apartment. I'm happy to answer any questions you may have.
Is there any parking? – There is no parking in my building. However, there is a parking garage within walking distance. There is a daily parking fee of $10. You will be charged $15 daily if you wish to come and go.
Are the stairs to your apartment steep? – While the stairs here are steeper than most, I guarantee that no guest has ever fallen. My guests have included children and elderly couples, and none of them have ever had trouble using the stairs.
Is there a hair dryer? – Absolutely. In the bathroom, there is an excellent hairdryer in the cabinet.
Please don't hesitate to contact me if you need further

assistance. Thank you, and I look forward to meeting you!
Kind regards,

Kay

Write your response as simply as possible. Make sure that your answers are concise but thorough enough to address any questions. Ultimately, you want to provide them with all the information they need to make an instant reservation.

If you receive questions, consider them as a sign that you left out relevant information on your listing. When possible, include this information in your listing.

Here is a sample message I send to guests after a booking is confirmed:

Dear Mary,
Thank you for booking with me! I am delighted to have you as my guest, and I am sure you will have a memorable time in Miami.
I will send you all the information you need to make your stay memorable, such as:
• Directions to my apartment
• Guidelines on how to use my electronics and equipment

• A local guide of places to visit in the area. In the meantime, feel free to contact me if you have any questions. You can reach me via email (email address) or by phone (phone number).

Last but not least, if you have already booked your travel, I would appreciate knowing when you will arrive and how you will get here. Please include your airline name and flight number if you plan to arrive by plane. So, I can give you a timely welcome! Have a safe trip.

Kind regards,

Kay

After sending the above message, I send over a set of detailed instructions and a copy of my guidebook. Making your visitors feel at home from the moment they arrive is the key to a stellar review.

I contact my guests once more the day before they are due to arrive to confirm the arrival time and date. I also ask if they need assistance with their bags.

I strongly recommend following this guideline. Providing your guests with an unforgettable experience will help you stand out from the crowd. The result is a win-win scenario. Guests will feel much more relaxed and welcomed when you put in a bit of time and effort.

In the event that something goes wrong during their stay, this level of service will make your guests more likely to leave a positive review. Eventually, you will want to automate guest communication. I will elaborate on that later.

PROVIDE GUESTS WITH INFORMATION ABOUT THE LOCAL SCENE

You've visited the nightclubs, eaten at the best restaurants, and lounged in the coffee shops. You know your city like the back of your hand. Take a moment to think about that. This is your chance to share your valuable knowledge with newcomers.

I recommend that you provide a list of exciting activities and dining options with:

- A photo
- A map and address
- A menu link (if food is served)
- The best time of day to visit

Places to include:

- Dining establishments
- Bars and clubs
- Transportation options

- Malls and shops nearby
- Supermarkets nearby
- Drugstores
- Places of interest

ANTICIPATE THE NEEDS OF YOUR GUESTS

Your guests want a place where they feel at home. A great host makes their space feel welcoming and relaxing. One of my favorite places that I stayed when using Airbnb was a spacious apartment on the Venezuelan coast of Playa El Yaque.

I rented out an apartment near the beach with several friends. The location was excellent, and the host was incredibly gracious, but the amenities made the stay unforgettable. We had a fully-equipped kitchen with a wide range of appliances, a washing machine, a fully-stocked linen closet, and three televisions with Netflix access. It was pretty sweet.

Why did it seem so different? It was the little touches. Or maybe it was the sense of comfort that crossed international borders. I felt an overwhelming sense of calm when I first entered the apartment. I felt instantly at ease. As a host, you are responsible for creating a warm and welcoming environment for every guest.

GO BEYOND THE BASICS

You will be well on your way to obtaining excellent reviews if you follow the suggestions I have already given you. However, if you want to provide a five-star experience and the highest level of service, you have to go above and beyond. Here are some suggestions.

- Provide them with a local SIM card and a cell phone.
- Offer them coupons for local sights, nightlife, and restaurants
- Provide a selection of local restaurant menus
- Provide bicycles for your guests
- Provide public transport cards
- Pick up guests at the airport

THE LITTLE THINGS MATTER

Quality service is not just about what is offered but also how it is delivered. I assume most people have seen *Cupcake Wars?* Although high-quality ingredients and delicious sweets are a must, what really separates quality from mediocre is aesthetics. The color scheme, balance, and the overall aesthetic of the arrangement are all important. Presentation is equally important in the short-term rental business as it is in competitive baking.

Here are a few tips to make your home look as opulent as a luxury resort:

- Folded towels with shampoo and conditioner bottle
- Mints or sweets on the bed with a welcome note
- Wine or champagne
- Fruit bowl on the kitchen table

BE RESPONSIVE

Although it would be ideal if guests did not have any questions or concerns during their stay, that most likely won't be the case.

Rather than worrying about whether they'll have questions, think about how you can ensure a satisfying experience. Providing guests a straightforward way to communicate during their stay and offering them value will result in more 5-star reviews.

Asking guests directly for their opinions is the best way to get them to share their thoughts. You should, however, be careful not to bombard them with messages. Keep them brief, polite, and not too frequent.

Keep in touch with your guests by following these suggestions:

Send a Message to Guests After Check-in

After your guests have settled in, after two to three hours, simply say:

> Hi Mary! Just checking to make sure everything is okay and you're settled in. Please do not hesitate to contact me with any questions. I am available by phone or text.
> Thanks,
>
> Kay

Contact Your Guests Every two to Three Days

If guests are staying for a while, be sure to communicate every second or third day with a quick note. Consider including relevant information in your follow-up message to make it sound more natural. For example:

Hi Mary, just letting you know that Collins Avenue
will be closed tomorrow. Please use 43rd st instead. I
hope all is well. Don't hesitate to get in touch.
Thanks,

Kay

When your guests feel comfortable speaking with you directly, they are less likely to keep their grievances to themselves. They are also less likely to include them in their review.

If Something Goes Wrong, Make it Right

Each guest's level of unhappiness will be different. Some dissatisfied travelers will point out minor issues, while others will be so dissatisfied with the interior they will leave right away. Whether or not you can resolve the issue and make your guest happy depends on the situation. If you can't fix the problem, you can still save your reputation if you handle the situation correctly.

When a guest has a problem, you should first determine if it can be rectified. I fix problems as soon as I find them. Problems that are easily fixed are rarely a cause for concern as long as they are resolved quickly. Timely responses will be viewed favorably. In addition, if you respond immediately, you may receive a more favorable review than you would have otherwise!

Despite your apartment being spotless and neatly arranged, you may encounter a guest who does not believe it is up to standard. If this happens, you have several options. The guest should be offered a refund only if they refrain from leaving a comment. You can charge the guest, but you should consider the potential harm to your business from a poor review. Since these incidents will be few and far between, the best thing to do is to maintain your reputation and safeguard your future earnings.

As an Airbnb host, you're part of the hospitality industry and should always put your guests first. When you go the extra mile to make your guests' stay extraordinary, they will tell their family and friends about it.

AUTOMATION IS KEY

As a host, you're always looking for ways to streamline your processes and reduce the time you spend on them. Airbnb automation can help you do that. Automation can save you up to 70% of the time you spend performing routine tasks (iGMS, 2021). Every day, the rental business becomes more competitive. Airbnb owners face many challenges. It's no surprise that automation is becoming more and more popular in dealing with the workload.

Automating your business can give it a second wind and even help it generate more money. A single listing will earn you $1,000/month, but you want 20 listings earning you $20,000/month! It's possible! Here are a few ways you can use automation to scale your rental arbitrage business and make big profits.

Messages Should be Automated

There are ways to automate communication with guests, such as answering their messages before, during, and after their stay. You can outsource it to a virtual assistant for $5 an hour. Essentially, you're paying yourself $5 an hour to do it yourself. Consider whether it is worthwhile to communicate with guests in-house or to outsource the task.

When handling guest communications, a virtual assistant can be extremely helpful. Most of the time, the virtual assistant will only charge for the time spent answering guests' questions, which keeps the overall cost to a minimum.

If you want to spend less time on guest communication, consider using software and a virtual assistant since using a program alone will have limitations. A guest might ask, "How do I set the thermostat?" Most programs won't provide an appropriate response. Guests, who are curious about "What's the wiFi?" There are several software programs available that are useful. A virtual assistant will be needed when a question is more complex or unique.

Automated Cleaning

Airbnb hosts often outsource the cleaning and turnover of their properties. Every time a guest checks out, cleaners visit your property and give it a thorough cleaning. A typical cleaning service includes everything from cleaning the rooms to washing linens and replenishing supplies like toilet paper, tissues, and shampoo. Cleaning services can relieve you of a lot of work. Another benefit of hiring a cleaning service is that it is one of the few jobs you must be present for. You can focus on other hosting duties by having someone else handle the task.

After you hire your cleaners, you will need to train them. Decide what is non-negotiable and what your needs are. Inform your cleaning staff of those items that are non-negotiable. Instructions should be provided for tasks requiring more technical knowledge or specific skills. Prepare a checklist before they start cleaning so they won't forget anything.

It might be a wise idea to do a couple of cleanings with them so you can discuss everything and make sure they understand your needs. You can't tell a cleaner to just clean because they'll end up doing it their own way. Miscommunications can happen, or you may forget to include something on your list. Your goals can be clearly communicated by being there in person and staying with them during a couple of cleanings.

Once you have supervised the cleaners a few times, you can let them work independently and then conduct your own quality control checks. To ensure the work is still done to the same standard even if you aren't there.

Your guests will also provide you with feedback. Ask them if they are satisfied with your property. If you use a virtual assistant, ask them to follow up with guests about their experience. If there are any problems, inform your cleaners and resolve the issue as soon as possible to avoid negative reviews.

Automate the Exchange of Keys

It doesn't matter how you choose to automate the check-in process, as long as it works consistently. You don't want it to malfunction, making it difficult for guests to access the property. There are several options for automating the check-in process, each offering varying levels of security and trustworthiness.

▷ A Professional key Exchange Service

This option is a blend of traditional check-in methods with self-check-in methods. Key exchangers act as liaisons between the host and the guest. With key exchange services, you can provide a convenient location for picking up and dropping off keys, monitor the exchange of keys online, and even automate keyless entry.

▷ Lock box

Despite being the least technologically advanced option, lockboxes are the most reliable. A lockbox is attached to a doorknob or railing, and guests open it by entering a code or using a key.

▷ Smart Lock

Smart locks can be controlled remotely, usually by a smartphone app or by entering a password.

BECOME A SUPERHOST

Airbnb recognizes hosts for achieving certain standards through a variety of designations, the most prominent being "Superhost."

Superhosts are the platform's most successful, consistent, and professional hosts. Superhosts benefit from increased traffic to their listings, leading to increased bookings. In order to become a Superhost, you must perform well in several categories.

A Superhost provides exceptional service to their guests and adheres to a set of standards set by Airbnb. The requirements include completing a certain number of reservations, maintaining a high response rate, a low cancellation rate, and getting five-star reviews.

A host's eligibility to become a Superhost is evaluated every three months on the first day of each calendar quarter (January, April, July, and October) (Tom & Tom, 2021). Following a review, if you meet the requirements within the last 12 months, you are eligible for the Superhost title.

However, you won't be a Superhost immediately, even if you meet all the requirements. To qualify for the Superhost title, you will need to wait until the next review date when Airbnb reviews all listings. When it comes to being a Superhost, you don't need to have a certain number of reviews. Instead, you must maintain an average overall rating of 4.8 or better.

HOW TO GET 5-STAR REVIEWS & BOOST YOUR LISTING

Send Check-in and Check-out Messages

Communicate with your guests before, during, and after their stay. Be available to them and respond to their needs. Check-in and check-out are straightforward processes, but a mishandled one can ruin the entire experience. Don't forget that guests arriving for the first time may just have finished a long and exhausting journey. You never want them to wait outside your property for a long time.

Set Expectations

Is the property's appearance and atmosphere accurately portrayed in the photos? Is the apartment equipped with the appliances and amenities mentioned in the listing? Are the shops nearby as described? Make sure the listing describes the property accurately. Be careful not to make any promises you can't keep.

Address Issues Promptly and Seriously

Guests are your customers. And we all know the saying, "the customer is always right." This applies to your guests as well. Dissatisfied guests will write a negative review that other potential guests will see. According to Airbnb, approximately 70% of guests leave feedback

(Rusteen, 2019). Unhappy guests can negatively affect your earnings for months. You should resolve any issues as soon as possible. In addition, pretend that the issue is more pressing than the guest thinks. Everyone has a different perspective, and each guest will have different expectations. It may not matter to one guest if there is a piece of hair on the bed, but another may feel the house needs to be cleaned thoroughly.

Quickly get Your Guests Settled in

Make sure your guests are settled in your Airbnb as quickly as possible so they can start enjoying their vacation. In addition to providing details about the property, the guidebook can also help guests locate nearby points of interest (cafe, supermarket, health club), promote local events (painting classes, summer activities for children like story time), and learn regional slang.

I have put in a lot of effort to provide the best hosting experience. Fortunately, I have received positive feed-back and excellent ratings from my guests. Because I own multiple properties, I generally cannot personally greet all my guests. Despite this, I am still able to achieve excellent results with the right automation systems in place.

In the end, the best way to get positive reviews is to establish a solid and honest relationship with your guests. How can you do this? By being a great host.

Make sure you rate your guests as well! Asking for positive reviews in advance is an effective strategy.

I usually write my reviews within 24 hours of check-out. In addition, I always send a personal note to each guest. Here is an example:

> *Dear Mary,*
> *Thank you for being such a wonderful guest! I hope you enjoyed your stay in Miami. If you decide to visit again, you are always welcome!*
> *P.S. Since you were such a gracious guest, I have gone ahead and written you a glowing review!*

Be sure to mention that you wrote a very positive review. This is especially important because guests will not be able to read reviews unless they have submitted their own.

FIND MORE PROPERTIES

Once you've settled into your first property, the next step is to expand. Remember to be patient and trust the journey. Even if you live in an area popular with

Airbnbs, your first few months will most likely not be busy. Many people, however, enjoy staying in different Airbnbs and discovering new things to do.

The majority of hosts only have one listing. One listing is fine if you don't plan to grow your business. However, consider how much you would need to charge guests to earn a six-figure income from just one unit. If you don't have a large house, you may have problems. You should gradually add more listings to build a solid income. You should not do everything at once because it can be overwhelming. When you have a good grasp of the business, your property has an occupancy rate of 80% or more, and you are confident that adding another listing is a good idea, follow the same steps and find more properties.

If you want to be successful with your Airbnb listing, you must also have a business mindset. Listing properties is just one aspect of Airbnb. Airbnb hosts have only one listing on average, and three out of four listings generate less than $10,000 a year in rental income (Cave, 2017). On the other hand, Airbnb's most successful hosts make a lot of money, earning profits from most of the bookings the site receives each day. The most successful Airbnb business owners account for only 8% of all listings on the platform, but they earn nearly 20% of all booking revenue earned through the platform (Cave, 2017). How do they do it? They have a strong business sense and are skilled at running their listings efficiently.

Ideally, you won't be satisfied with just one rental, and with each property you rent, you'll be able to earn enough money to fund your next venture. Short-term rental properties can bring you a lot of income, and the more properties you own, the more income you can expect each month.

The owners of successful Airbnb rental arbitrage businesses consistently build long-term relationships with landlords that lead to successful deals. It is more than just a phone call. Make an effort to understand what the other party wants from their business and how you can help. This may seem simple, but it isn't done enough. Anyone can close a deal, but if you want to succeed with Airbnb rentals, you should focus on building relationships with landlords.

You will learn that successful people on Airbnb have one thing in common: they are driven to succeed and make money. They are driven to create wealth. A winning attitude motivates you to strive for more. You are constantly looking for ways to improve your business management and ensure that everything runs smoothly in order to maximize your income and minimize your expenses. Many, if not all, of these entrepreneurs, automate their Airbnb operations to accomplish this. You can save time and resources by using Airbnb automated management systems to help you manage your properties. Repairs and cleaning can also be outsourced and scheduled accordingly.

TOOLS TO TAKE YOUR BUSINESS TO THE NEXT LEVEL

Managing multiple Airbnb listings can be overwhelming. Cleaning and payments are just a few of the many tasks. Airbnb host tools make things easier. You should begin using these tools after you have listed at least five properties.

Property Management System

Bookings and keeping track of hosts are easier with a property management system. You can consolidate all your Airbnb accounts, create one dashboard and integrate multiple listings, provide automatic communication, transactions, data management, and a lot more. Co-hosting is another option.

Dynamic Pricing App

Increasing your Airbnb rental income is as simple as optimizing your pricing, as we have discussed previously. Automatically pricing your rental rates is the fastest and easiest way to increase your earnings and give you more time for yourself.

Cleaning Coordination Software

When you hire cleaners or a cleaning service, cleaning coordination software can save you a lot of time. You can schedule cleanings as well as create and monitor your supplies. It can also be integrated with your property management system.

Payment Processor

Since most short-term rental reservations are made electronically, accepting credit card payments online would be beneficial. AirBnb provides its own payment processor, but if you want to accept direct reservations, you can use a payment gateway like PayPal or Stripe.

Digital Guidebook

The purpose of the digital guidebook is straightforward: to provide guests with an unforgettable experience filled with local attractions they might not otherwise come across. You, as an Airbnb host, are in a great place to provide guests with these experiences. When an Airbnb guest heads to Canyon Point in Utah or Big Sur in California, thanks to the guidance of their host, they can experience the area like a local, and learn about the way of life. In addition, your digital guidebook will include instructions on how to check in and house rules.

SETTING UP YOUR BUSINESS FOR SUCCESS

You need to hire the right people to get your business off to a good start. Outsourcing is the process of hiring someone else to perform work you are not capable of doing or do not want to do. It can be more efficient to have someone else handle a particular task. The important thing to understand is that by not paying someone else to do the job, you will be keeping yourself free to perform higher level jobs. You shouldn't do it if you aren't getting paid enough for your time.

You can outsource a variety of tasks, such as cleaning, guest communication, co-hosting (if you choose that option), and maintenance.

Consider the following factors when deciding which tasks to outsource:

- Finding the right person or people is crucial.
- They must be trained to deliver results according to your specifications.

You must ensure that they have the tools and systems they need to meet your standards consistently.

Cleaning Service

Automating your Airbnb cleaning allows you to focus on other aspects of your business. There is no need to worry that some might turn off your guests.

An Airbnb cleaning company is the way to go. You can trust a cleaning company to maintain your apartment in a professional manner, just like a first-class hotel. In order to ensure that your Airbnb property is always pristine and ready to welcome guests, you need to hire professional cleaners who are familiar with Airbnb cleaning.

Co-Hosts

Multiple Airbnb listings can be overwhelming at times. Maintaining multiple properties, booking reservations, and accommodating multiple guests can be challenging. It can be challenging, but Airbnb has made it possible to have a co-host.

If you co-host an Airbnb listing, you hire someone to manage your listings. Co-hosts are responsible for maintaining Airbnb properties on behalf of Airbnb hosts. The co-host takes the pressure off of you, ensuring a smooth Airbnb experience. Isn't that great?

Your best option is to have a family member, friend, or other close associate help you manage your Airbnb properties. Co-hosting is beneficial if you have someone you trust and know.

Handyman

How do you handle repairs and upkeep if you aren't handy, don't have time, or don't live near your properties? Life is full of ups and downs. There are leaky pipes. The washing machine stops working. Maintenance needs to be done. In a lot of cases, these repairs will be the responsibility of the landlord, however, in order to maintain good reviews and attract new customers, you need to keep your property looking fabulous, so having a back-up option is key.

Hire a local handyman to handle your repairs. You will save a significant amount of money by avoiding high fees associated with property management. Handymen are significantly less expensive than property management services or general contractors. Airbnb rentals require maintenance on a regular basis. Every property will have a problem at some point. In general, it's not a good idea to hire a general contractor for a small problem. It's not worth the money. A handyman can handle all the little jobs for you at an affordable price without requiring you to spend a lot of time and effort doing them yourself.

Set Up a Standardized Process for Everything

Managing your property involves the most work in the beginning. This is when you are manually determining your listing prices, selecting and training your house-keeping and front desk staff, and establishing systems to ensure they perform to your standards.

To grow your business, employees need a clear understanding of your processes and adhere to them as closely as possible. It is your responsibility to ensure that all parties are aware of the process.

IT DOESN'T COME WITHOUT RISKS

Starting a business involves some risks. Having your first guests can be nerve-wracking. Just know, no matter how much planning you do, you can never be completely prepared. However, the way you approach situations determines whether or not your business will succeed. Airbnb hosts who build their businesses into six-figure incomes react to every situation rationally and pragmatically. Even when it's difficult for them to deal with their guests, they remember to be courteous and polite. They ensure guests are treated fairly. They have a "guests are always right" mindset, but they also have a "this is my business" mindset. To succeed in business, you need to strike the right balance between these two perspectives. However, you can't achieve this overnight. Developing this mindset takes time.

The key to managing risk is to recognize undesirable guests, such as rude individuals who might pose a threat to your property. While these guests may seem like your typical guests, they can sometimes give subtle indications that they are not concerned with leaving your Airbnb in a good state. They party in your home and ignore your guidelines. Setting rules for your Airbnb and enforcing them consistently is the best way to limit undesirable guests.

COMMON MISTAKES TO AVOID

Many things need to be considered when you first start hosting on Airbnb. It may take a while for you to see the success you want, so it is important you learn from the mistakes I made at the beginning of my journey. By learning the most common errors Airbnb hosts make, will improve your listings and increase bookings.

Unprofessional Listing

The worst thing you can do on Airbnb is have a listing that looks unprofessional. Bookings are based on first impressions, and if you mess up on the listing, nobody will be interested in booking your property.

Here are some common mistakes to avoid:

- An incomplete listing
- Listing title is generic and boring
- Having a bad cover photo
- Your listing description is lacking

You will increase your Airbnb property's appeal to guests if you pay attention to these factors.

Unattractive Photos

When listing on Airbnb, I recommend taking high-quality photos rather than snapping quick photos with your smartphone. A poor setup, poor lighting, and unflattering angles won't help you market your space.

The least you can do to make your Airbnb photos look good is to use a professional camera, take pictures under natural light (pictures at night are nice), and arrange your rental to reflect how you envision your ideal vacation rental.

Not Utilizing Airbnb's Filters

Would you prefer a one-night Friday booking or a three-day weekend stay? Airbnb now allows you to communicate your preferences and filter out guests who don't fit your criteria. A guest booking one night can ruin your long bookings, so you should set the filter to set a minimum of three days. You can set different filters on Airbnb and avoid wasting time. To increase profits, you need only the best guests.

Inadequate Pricing Strategy

The most common mistake new Airbnb hosts make is pricing their properties incorrectly. In most cases, this occurs when they fail to account for peak and off-peak seasons, as well as holiday periods. Let's say there is a special event happening in your neighborhood. You might want to increase your prices by $20-50 during that time. Increasing your prices during major holidays is also a good idea. Additionally, if your prices are too high, you could lose bookings. Pricing is very important in the hospitality industry.

Not Understanding the Importance Of Reviews

Hosts who don't recognize the importance of reviews are doing themselves a disservice. Negative reviews are just as bad as none at all. Positive reviews help you rank higher in search results. To get there, you will have to ask your guests to review your space. If you neglect to do so, you may lose the opportunity of becoming a Super Host. Remember, to let the guest know you reviewed him so he will be encouraged to do the same.

Ignoring the Competition

Keeping an eye on your local competition is crucial. Make sure you:

- Keep an eye on their prices regularly.
- Take a close look at their photos.
- Try to make a reservation with one of them or at least book a refundable space and see how they treat prospective guests.

You can determine what improvements your business needs by staying aware of your competition and analyzing them.

Also, it's interesting to see how the market reacts when new players enter the market. Sometimes, they won't last, so you need to find out why, and usually you can do that by looking at their pictures, prices, and reviews.

Lack of Hospitality

Failing to communicate effectively with your guests is the worst mistake you can commit as an Airbnb host. Respond as soon as possible to any questions you receive from a prospective guest. Airbnb will also penalize you if you take longer than 24 hours to respond. One of the most crucial aspects of messaging is setting the right tone and responding to potential guests' questions thoroughly.

Managing Everything Alone

Professional services for Airbnb are there for a reason —they're experts. That means they will run their business efficiently and to the highest standard. In my opinion an Airbnb host's biggest mistake is to attempt to do everything. It's likely you might not clean as well as a professional would, and this may negatively affect guests' satisfaction. Airbnb hosts can delegate so many things to others, such as cleaning, exchanging keys, and maintaining listings across multiple platforms.

CONCLUSION

Whatever the future holds, one thing is for sure. Short-term accommodation is redefining the industry with the demand for more personalized travel experiences. The power balance has shifted from the host to the traveler.

While serving as UN World Tourism Organization Secretary-General, Taleb Rifai encouraged the hotel industry to embrace this trend to remain competitive (World Tourism Organization, 2017). Hotels have invested heavily in new business models because they know they must adapt or risk losing out on business. For example, Accor Group invested in Onefinestay, an online hosting service that caters to travelers looking for private accommodations with the same amenities as a high-end hotel. They also own Oasis Properties, a company specializing in properties with distinctive architectural features and décor.

Hotels and cruise lines around the world are incorporating local knowledge into their marketing strategies. Marriott has invested in PlacePass, a tour and activity booking service, and Royal Caribbean Cruises owns GoBe, a company that provides unique excursions.

Many hotels, motels, and bed and breakfasts now offer accommodations through hosting platforms like Airbnb. And Airbnb is expanding its offerings. It has launched a premium tier that targets high-spenders looking for an adventurous experience without sacrificing the amenities they expect from a hotel.

Airbnb hosts only have a small percentage of the short-term housing market. In 2016, Pew Research Center reported that less than one in nine Americans stayed in a private home booked through an online hosting platform (Smith, 2016). The majority of Americans are unfamiliar with short-term housing platforms. Host platforms are increasingly popular among university graduates and newly wealthy individuals. The median age of home-sharing users in the United States is 42 (Phys.org, 2016). However, wealthy baby boomers are starting to follow the young and hip trend.

Still, there is a long way to go. As hosting platforms market their brands more aggressively, their popularity is expected to increase. Private listings dominate the market in Europe and North America, but Asia is experiencing the fastest growth.

The bar has been raised thanks to Airbnb, and everyone has a chance to prosper. Travelers are increasingly opting for culturally immersive tours led by local guides. And now Airbnb allows hosts to offer city tours, culinary experiences, and so much more.

I keep my focus on what I do best—earning money renting out my properties to travelers around the world while giving back to my community. I am not the same person I was a few years ago, and neither is my business. It has grown exponentially. However, I remain committed to providing guests with an experience that I would enjoy myself. When I receive a fruit basket or an excited message saying, "I wish I could stay forever," it makes me feel proud and successful!

I'm making new friends and having a good time. My income allows me to take luxurious trips around the world and spend time with my family.

The expectations of travelers have increased since short-term housing was a bare-bones operation. Hosts can make their listings more attractive, their prices more affordable, and their spaces more welcoming so their guests feel more at home. By doing so, you will join the ranks of thousands of Airbnb arbitrage business owners who are reaping the benefits of hosting travelers.

As a brand new host, I hope this book will help you get started with your listing and maximize your earnings. Some of the top Airbnb hosts started out in humble circumstances but have managed to achieve success through hard work and perseverance. A large proportion of high-income earners invest in real estate. With Airbnb arbitrage, you can earn a lot of money without owning any property. However, it is important to cultivate a good relationship with your landlord so that they can understand the benefits of allowing you to list their property on Airbnb. Don't forget they will also benefit from your success, and before you know it, you'll have a very successful partnership. The next step is to make more connections with new landlords. Keep going to grow your Airbnb arbitrage empire.

And remember location, location, location. Before investing in a particular area, thoroughly research the market. Study the demographics and challenges short-term renters face. If you set your business apart from your competitors, Airbnb arbitrage can be a lucrative business. Airbnb can take you far. If you are determined, you can make a significant impact from the second you list your first place on Airbnb to the point where you start bringing in substantial income from several properties. Scaling and listing multiple properties are the keys to success and a big bank account. Be patient. Learning the Airbnb system takes time, and you must be persistent. If you try to do too many things at once, you may lose sight of your main objectives. As a host, you have a voice in what travel and tourism should look like. It's only up from here!

REFERENCES

7 Airbnb SEO Tips for Airbnb Entrepreneur | iGMS. (2016, December 15). IGMS. https://www.igms.com/airbnb-seo/

Airbnb Automation: 7 Ways To Put Your Business on Autopilot. (2021, June 1). IGMS. https://www.igms.com/automate-airbnb/

Airbnb Experiences: A New Way to Increase Your Airbnb Income | iGMS. (2018, June 13). IGMS. https://www.igms.com/airbnb-experiences/

Airbnb host fined £100,000 for letting council flat. (2019, July 29). *BBC News.* https://www.bbc.com/news/technology-49149983

Airbnb Rental Arbitrage: FAQ and Money-making Guide. (2020, January 30). IGMS. https://www.igms.com/airbnb-rental-arbitrage/ #What_Is_the_Formula_for_Successful_Airbnb_Arbitrage *Average Airbnb Prices By City: What Should You Charge For Your Airbnb?* (n.d.). AllTheRooms Analytics. https://www.alltherooms.com/analytics/average-airbnb-prices-by-city/

Aydin, R. (2019, September 20). How 3 guys turned renting air mattresses in their apartment into a $31 billion company, Airbnb. Business Insider. https://www.businessinsider.com/how-airbnb-was-founded-a-visual-history-2016-2?r=US&IR=T

Cave, A. (2017, November 29). *The 75 People Who Make $1M A Year From Airbnb.* Lance Edwards Deals & Dollars Club | Commercial Real Estate Tips. https://dealsanddollarsclub.com/the-75-people-who-make-1m-a-year-from-airbnb/

Editor, T. (2017, September 7). *Airbnb now has more room listings than the top 5 hotel brands combined.* TOPHOTELNEWS. https://tophotel.news/airbnb-now-has-more-room-listings-than-the-top-5-hotel-brands-combined/

How to Create an Outstanding Airbnb Listing [A Full Guide]. (2020, October 8). IGMS. https://www.igms.com/airbnb-listing/

Kamp, G. (2022, March 30). *How to Create the Perfect Airbnb Bedroom (with product links!)*. Gretchen Kamp. https://www.gretchenkamp. com/blog/airbnb-bedroom

Kaylee. (2019, August 8). *4 Simple Tricks to Cut Your Airbnb Energy Bill.* Neome. https://www.neome.co/post/4-simple-tricks-to-cut-your-airbnb-energy-bill

Lavie, J. (2020, January 21). *Airbnb kitchen essentials: Preparing a cooking space that guests will love to use.* GuestReady's Airbnb Hosting Blog. https://www.guestready.com/blog/airbnb-kitchen-essentials/

Rusteen, D. (2019, November 10). *5 Tips to 5-Star Airbnb Reviews.* OptimizeMyBnb.com. https://optimizemyairbnb.com/5-tips-5-star-airbnb-reviews/

Smartbnb. (2021, December 13). *Instant Booking on Airbnb: How to Use It Effectively? | Hospitable.com.* Hospitable. https://hospitable.com/instant-booking-airbnb/

Smith, A. (2016). *FOR MEDIA OR OTHER INQUIRIES.* http://assets. pewresearch.org/wp-content/uploads/sites/14/2016/05/PI_2016. 05.19_Sharing-Economy_FINAL.pdf

Symon He. (2020). *Airbnb for dummies.* John Wiley & Sons. *The Airbnb Host's Living Room Essentials Checklist.* (2018, June 8). BnbNomad. https://bnbnomad.com/airbnb-living-room-checklist/

The Best Cities for Airbnb: Compare Markets Side by Side | AirDNA. (2019, December 6). AirDNA - Short-Term Vacation Rental Data and Analytics. https://www.airdna.co/blog/best-cities-for-airbnb

Thomas, A. (2018, February 26). *The Secret Ratio That Proves Why Customer Reviews Are So Important.* Inc.com; Inc. https://www.inc. com/andrew-thomas/the-hidden-ratio-that-could-make-or-break-your-company.html

Tom, & Tom. (2021, February 16). *How to Become a Superhost on Airbnb – and Maintain It.* Host Tools. https://hosttools.com/blog/airbnb-rentals/become-airbnb-superhost/?swcfpc=1

Universe, A. (2018, December 5). *8 Airbnb Bathroom Essentials - The Ultimate Step-By-Step Guide.* Airbnb Hosting Tips. https://airbnbuni verse.com/airbnb-bathroom-essentials/

US warms to "sharing" services like Uber, Airbnb. (2016). https://phys.org/ pdf382866229.pdf

Vacation Rental Market Size, Share Analysis Report, 2020-2027. (n.d.). www.grandviewresearch.com. https://www.grandviewresearch. com/industry-analysis/vacation-rental-market

world tourism organization. (2017). https://sustainabledevelopment.un. org/content/documents/2622annual_report_2016_web_0.pdf

Zaragoza, R. (2021, November 12). *Airbnb Rental Arbitrage: The Complete Guide.* Investment Property Tips | Mashvisor Real Estate Blog. https://www.mashvisor.com/blog/airbnb-rental-arbitrage/

Made in the USA
Las Vegas, NV
23 February 2024

86192593R00107